The Turns in Life

John Frye

To Mark
Best Wishes
John Frye
2-20-14

i

Bible verses are from The King James Bible.

Acknowledgements:

I would like to give a special thanks to Arliss Dickerson and Kerri Bennett for their help in getting this book to print. Also a special thanks to my wife, Sue, and my daughter in law, Shannon Beckwith Frye, for their time and effort in working with me on the final content.

Contents

Introduction

My wife, Linda Sue Porter Frye, and I attend Christian Valley Christian Church (CVCC) located in Jonesboro, AR. My only son, Jonathan and his wife, Shannon Beckwith Frye, also live there. They have two children. They are my pride and joy. I hope they realize how much that I love them. Their names are Joshua Caleb, age 13 and Jillian Kate, age 7. They also attend Christian Valley Christian Church.

Sue and I became members of this church a few years ago and have met many new Christian friends. We have a group called "The Senior Saints." Barbara and Greyson Sanders are the host of this group. Thank you Sanders family for your great work and hospitality. We meet monthly and enjoy the fellowship. In November of each year, we take a trip to Branson, MO for shopping. We also take in a few shows. Everyone always has a great time.

J.D. and Inez Salmons are a precious couple in this group. J.D. is a special friend of mine. We certainly have our laughs together. During one of our breakfast outings J.D. talked about how bad things were when he was growing up and how poor he was. I thought about my own life and was inspired to write this book. J.D. went on and on about his hard times. I compared our lives in the early years. There is no doubt that J.D. went through some very difficult years. But I just had to tell him some of my childhood adventures. I told him I appreciated his stories, for I had grown up on the very poor side of the tracks also. Then we went on to trade tales, and we got pretty carried away. I believe that he thought that I was just kidding about the way we lived in the difficult early years, but it was all true.

I think that everyone who knows J.D. has a lot of respect for him. Every Sunday morning you will find him shaking hands and greeting as many people as he can at church. J.D. tells everyone that I am his buddy, and I consider this an honor. He gave me the idea for writing this book. So hold on to your seat J.D.; here we go!

The early years were very harsh for most people. I remember what a bumpy road I had to travel to get to where I am today. I can truthfully say that if I had gone only a degree to the right or the left, I would not be writing this book. I think that most people could say the same thing about their journeys in life. There are many decisions in life that can change your entire journey. The career you choose, your soul mate, or your friends you come in contact with can all play a major factor in who you become. Our families also play a tremendous role in our pathways of life. Why are we born into a certain family? Just think about comparing our lives with someone who is born into a Royal family. What a deal!

I think that the negative things in our lives are much easier to remember than the good things. I guess that's because of the impact these things have on our growth process. It seems that we must go through certain things in life to get to where God wants us to be. God had a great deal to do with my growth into manhood. It seems that I have always known there was a God. I just had to find a unique way for him to communicate with me. I had to determine what he wanted me to do in life and how I was to live it. I learned a quote once: "Prosperity comes to ordinary people and men of means and ability, but it is the prerogative of a great man to overcome the calamities and terrors which frighten ordinary mortals!" I think men must be tried by fire that they might find out who they are. God has a father's feelings, loves good men and says to them: by labors, sorrows, and privations let them be tried in order that they may gain real strength.

Ephesians 3:13

Wherefore I desire ye faint not at my tribulations for you, which is your Glory.

In my early childhood, my precious mother, was the only one in my family circle that had any recollection that there was a God. She believed that we should live a good life according to the rules of life. I cannot remember my parents ever attending church. All I could find out about my grandfather on my mother's side is that he drank a lot and was not much on religion. Everyone else was hell bent on doing whatever it took to have fun, except my youngest brother. Actually, he was nine years old when I was born.

After he grew older, he drank alcohol on some occasions, but, all in all, he was a fairly down-the-middle-of-the-road person. Everyone in my family except my mother and sister were very heavy smokers. These two were also nondrinkers. My family worked very hard. They didn't make much money and barely made a living. They seemed to feel like the world owed them a good time for all their hard work. They spent what little they had on a small amount of food and the rest on booze and tobacco. I think my mother was opposed to this action. She occasionally voiced her opinion, but she still tolerated it. After all, what else could she have done? I don't think there were any drugs way back then. There was only some medication from the doctor. We only went to visit him on rare occasions. We had to be really sick before we ever considered going to see a doctor. I think I was probably around six years old before I ever went to see one. This visit was for an ear infection, and I think the doctor treated me for free. We didn't have any money. My father blew cigarette smoke into my ear and said that this would make it all well. I have to say, it seemed to help to relieve the immediate pain and pressure. I don't think this was a good thing, but my family had some strange ideas about life. Please don't try this at home! I remember that most of the medicine that we took was Black Draft for the bowel problems, Exlax for the other bowel problems, Quinine for stomach ache, Grover's Chill tonic for fever, and all the Vicks Salve that you could stand. This Vicks Salve was for the common cold and the stopped up sinuses. Sometimes we had to eat some of the Vicks Salve for some unknown reason. After reviewing this medicine usage, I can see why I act the way I do today. I didn't have a chance to become normal – ha, ha.

I believe that we are creatures of habit. I am convinced that we need to set goals for our lives. We need to have a positive attitude about our goals and about life in general. We don't need to say that we need to exercise more but say that we exercise 30 minutes a day. Or we don't need to say that we watch too much TV but we have limited our TV viewing to 2 hours per day. We need to read something educational each day. We need to stay connected to friends, and certainly not just by social media. We need to pick up the phone or go visit them. Sometimes this can be just as good as a dose of good medicine. We need to put our actions on a timeline. Most successful people are extremely goal oriented.

A goal is only a good goal if it is 100% attainable and requires some physical action to obtain it. If we can stay healthy, the results can be more energy and fewer doctor bills. Therefore, we can say that health and wealth go hand in hand.

One of my goals in life is to have a positive attitude. I try to make the best of a bad situation. My glass is always half full. In other words, I believe in everyone until they prove me wrong. Some people's glass is half empty. They do not like you until you have proven yourself to them.

I enjoy being around happy people with a positive attitude. There is no room for depression. After all, God is always with us. Sometimes we tend to forget that he is there.

I Thessalonians 5:17

Pray without ceasing.

To me, this verse means that we should be in a prayerful state of mind, constantly. We should be able to pray at all times, anywhere, anytime. If you ever find yourself in a situation in which you cannot feel good about praying, then you need to flee this situation immediately. This is an indication of the presence of Satan.

God will help us with all of our decisions if we will only let him. I do not believe that this action is very difficult. When there is what I call "static" in a decision, and we cannot easily resolve it, then we need to reconsider our decision.

Chapter 1: The Journey

This journey of life begins at the turn of the century, in the early 1900's. My mother was born in 1905, and my father was born in1892. My mother was several years younger than my father. I was told that my father and mother were married, and I think this was true, even though I have never seen any form of marriage license. My father had been married before he met my mother, and he had some children. I have not had much success in finding out anything about him. His first wife, Nettie Brooks, may have had some connection to Arkansas. I guess that Daddy may have visited or lived in Arkansas for a while. I do not know why or how this marriage ended. I want to think there was a divorce or some legal separation. Who knows? Most of the names of my stepbrothers, according to some census papers that a friend in Maryland sent to me, were connected to my immediate family. There were first and middle names that were carried over to my father's marriage to my mother. There was a Louis Elmer Frye born in 1889. Then my older brother was born in 1925 and named Louis Barrett Frye. There was a George Lewis Butler Frye, and my next to oldest brother was Charles Butler Frye. There was a John William Franklin Frye, and my youngest brother was named William Eugene (Bill) Frye. There was also a John William Franklin Fry way back in the family tree born on September 29, 1861. I can relate to this name, since my name turned out to be John Franklin Frye. I have mostly gone by the nickname of Johnny. My older brother referred to me many times as John Henry.

We will never understand in this life, why we were born into a certain family. God only knows and maybe someday, if we need to know, God will reveal this process. Therefore, I will begin my story here.

The Frye name began with the spelling of Fry, and later the "e" was added. In some listings, I also found it spelled as Frey. My father was mainly a commercial fisherman. But, he would farm some during the farming season. The rest of the year, he sold the fish that he caught just to have enough money to barely get by. He was listed on the census form as a farmer. From what I have been able to figure out, he was just a drifter. He did some sharecropping later in life. He never owned any farmland, but just worked someone else's land. He was paid a monthly wage in advance for the crop that he produced from the land. Then, after the crop was harvested, the landlord settled up with him. This was never very much. This settlement was certainly not enough to live through to the next year. I guess this is why he took up fishing and selling them to buy food and strong drink. My family worked hard for very little pay, and they seemed to forget about any of life's trouble. They used the strong drink to drown out the thought of the next week's hard work. They were honest and friendly people, and they would not harm anyone. They liked to have company and made friends easily. They were a close-knit family and, if they committed to a chore, you could pretty well consider it done.

My mother had several brothers and sisters. Most of the boys worked for the railroad. This was a very good job with great pension benefits. Most of the mother's brothers-in-law also worked for the railroad. I remember there was one who worked for the post office. He had a peg leg. I don't know how he lost his leg. I will mention him again later.

George Pennington & Oss Harding

My grandfather, whom I met when I was very young, also worked on the railroad. It seems that this would have been a great job for my father. I remember him saying that he pursued the railroad job, once, and all they wanted him to do was to pull weeds from around the rails. This job paid real good money, and he certainly didn't have any. My father did not have enough patience for this job. He was more of a drifter, looking for the end of the rainbow pot of gold. Anyway, this would have been a **"Turn in Life"** direction for me, if he had worked many years for the railroad and retired with a nice pension.

I never got the opportunity to meet my grandmother. She was a homemaker. My grandfather visited his Arkansas daughter a couple of times. I don't think my grandmother ever came.

Grandma and Grandpa Wenner

To my findings, my parents, in the early years, did not live in a house. They lived in a tent on a riverbank located in Maryland. I visited this area later in my life. This visit was very interesting. Both of my parents had very little schooling, but they could read and write somewhat.

Mother and Dad had four boys and one girl. The first child was a boy, Louis Barrett; and the next was a girl, Louise Marie. These two were born in Maryland. Times were tough. No jobs, no house, no money; just a young family to care for. Looking back, it must have been just a way of life. This was common for most folks. Everyone just accepted that this was life, and they must endure. Things got so bad that my family had to make a very tough decision. You remember one of the life-changing or destined-to-survive decisions that I wrote about earlier? Well, without this decision, I could have been born in Maryland, which may not have been a bad thing; but this would have been a **"Turn in Life"** for me for sure. I will highlight these decisions as I write this book. I have based this entire book on these decisions. I call them **"The Turns in Life"**. These are life-changing or life-altering decisions. On some occasions, we may not even have any control of the situation. I think that everyone has some of these decisions to make in their lives.

With nothing to lose and with little to gain, my mother and father, with two children, I am told, boarded a train. I do not know if they had any idea where this train was headed. Maybe they knew that it was headed south and eventually into Arkansas. Remember... no money, therefore, no train ticket. They boarded the train without a ticket. Like hobos, I guess. Who knows? Back then, the train crew may have been aware of this type of rider. I don't think my family was the poorest in town, but I think they may have been right down there with the poorest. Having limited information, they must have headed toward Georgia. I have been led to believe that my next brother Charles (Buddy) Butler was born there. My mother talked a lot about him being born in a peach orchard. Upon his retirement, so that he could have social security, Buddy obtained a birth certificate from the state of Maryland. I don't think they had any real information about his birth. Things were done much differently way back then. The poor did not go to a doctor or a hospital for childbirth. They asked a friend to be what they called a "midwife". This was someone who hopefully had some childbirth experience.

The next time I can remember my mother saying anything about their life was when they arrived in Arkansas. My father signed the 1930's census form as a farmer located near England, AR. It seems that they worked on a farm for a few years. In 1935 my third brother, William (Bill) Eugene was born. I am assuming near England, AR. This would later prove to be a real blessing to me and my family, as he assumed head of the household early in his life. Times were tough. Most sharecroppers had very little. The landowner would get most of the money. It would have been great if my family would have been able to save enough or made some sort of deal to become a landowner, even if it would have been for only a small tract of land. This would be another one of those **"Turn in Life"** decisions for me. Each of my brothers and sister had some schooling. However, as was the custom back then, the children attended school only until they were old enough to work. In most cases, this would be farm work. Keep in mind that most of this was share cropping. There was no daily or weekly pay. They received a monthly advance on the crop. The total bill would be settled after the crop was harvested. The money earned was never enough to last until the next year.

Chapter 2: The Pastoria Move

The next move my family made was to Pastoria, AR. This was a very small town, really not even a town; it was just a place in the road with one general store. There was a lake called Pipkin Lake. This lake was named for the nearby landowner. It was fed by the Arkansas River. Each spring, the river would rise high enough to spill over into the lake and restock it with spawning fish. Therefore, my father decided to camp out or live on the banks of this lake. He caught fish to sell, and he did some farm work for the Pipkin family just to have enough money to barely get by. Of course, it didn't take very much for my family at the time. There was no house. They had obtained an old funeral home tent to live in. These tents were just for a covering. The sides did not extend all the way to the ground. I was told that my dad took some old barn boards and extended the sides all the way to the ground and then he placed some of the boards inside for the flooring. I do not know how long this type of living took place or if they lived through any wintertime conditions on Pipkin Lake.

About the time I was born in 1944, someone had to feel real sorry for my family. They offered us an old house to live in near this lake. I suppose it was the Pipkin family. I will be forever grateful for this act of kindness. This old house was located just over the levee from the Pipkin Lake. It was near a pit of water also fed by the Arkansas River and was called the "Blue Hole". There was a floodgate from the lake that regulated the lake's water level. When the floods came, the water from the lake would flow over into the "Blue Hole." Therefore, fish came through the floodgate and stocked this hole of water. It was very deep. Sometimes my family caught fish right here near the house. Fish was a special food for us. As a matter of fact, fish is still my favorite food today. However, some of these were certainly not the same variety that I like today. Although, we caught some nice catfish, most of them were sold, since they were the prime market fish. The buffalo fish was also high in value. It was good, with a sort of special sweet-fish taste. There was also, gar, grinnell, mud cats (pollywogs), and drum. The gar was ok, but you had to clean it in a special way. The meat had to be removed from the very hard outer shell. This was done with an ax to cut it into steaks. And then the gristle was removed from each steak cut. Not bad, they were just very difficult to prepare for cooking. If that was all you had, it seemed pretty good. The grinnell was very soft fish and had to be eaten hot. It chewed like cotton. The more you chewed it, the larger it would get. The pollywogs were a small yellow-green catfish that were very tough in nature, and most of them had a very strong fishy taste. These fish were not very good, but they were edible, and we ate them often. The drum had to be fairly large, or there would be too many small bones. They needed to come from fairly clear water or they would have a muddy taste. There was also crappie and bream, which could not be sold or even kept when they were caught by commercial means. We certainly enjoyed eating these whenever we caught them legally.

There were even a few turtles and many, many snakes. I cannot remember any snakes for food, but there was turtle. Some of the turtles were the soft-shelled turtle, and others were snapping turtles. The soft- shelled turtle was edible, and the snapping turtle or some called it the "loggerhead" turtle, was used for making soup. Doesn't that sound appetizing?

I need to mention there were no necessities present in our lives for many years. No running water. No bathroom. No washing machine. We used what was called an outhouse. This was common back then. All poor people had these. Even some of the landowners had these outhouses as well. Some were called "studios." Some even had a double hole or a "two seater" in case of more than one emergency. This was just a way of life for many, many years to come. There was no toilet tissue. We used old magazine pages. I can remember the Sears and Roebuck Catalogs were real popular. You just had to be very careful with the gloss-covered pages.

One year, we made a little extra money selling fish. Dad purchased a commercial fishing license, so he could have more ways to catch fish. He bought a gill net. He would set this net in a good area of the lake. As the fish swam into it, the smaller fish would pass through the mesh, and the gills of the larger fish would get caught in the net. Dad also used a hoop net to catch many fish. This was made with several large, circular hoops covered with netting. Dad would place some bait inside it. Then the fish would swim into the net through a small funnel-shaped opening. When they would attempt to swim out, it would be very difficult for them to locate the inverted funnel opening, so they were caught. Usually he would place this net in an area of the lake or river that had some current or some sort of water movement. He would frequently catch large numbers of fish using this method.

Dad also used snag lines. Only licensed commercial fishermen could use these lines. The hooks were extended from a large main line, and they were very close together so that when the fish would swim by, the snag hooks would catch them. We ordered most all of our fishing equipment from Adams Net and Twine Company in St. Louis, MO. All of the lines were made from cotton, and Dad soaked them in used motor oil for preservation. This was a mess, but it worked, for these lines would last for a long time before they had to be replaced.

We had a garden for fresh vegetables, some chickens and a hog or two. Now my family was living up to some sort of standard. They were now making it a little better than just getting by.

So, early in the morning, around 4 a.m. in 1944, I was born in the house by the "Blue Hole" near Pastoria, AR, with a colored midwife assisting the birth. At least my birth was at a time the family seemed to be getting life together. But this didn't last too many years. There were more hard times ahead. Some were common to this era, and others were brought on with bad decisions.

1944 was a year of tumult, a year of change...a year in which we could rejoice. That was the year that Mac Arthur began his drive through the Pacific Islands, and the groundwork was laid for a United Nations. The Allies invaded Normandy on June 6, marking the turning point for a World War II victory.

California beat Washington in the Rose Bowl; jockey Conn McCreary rode Pensive to the winner's circle in the Kentucky Derby, and the Detroit Red Wings pirated home the Stanley Cup. "Going My Way" won the Oscar for Best Picture, and ex-swimmer, Ester Williams became a star in *Bathing Beauty*, while Lauren Bacall opened in *To Have and Have Not*.

In the White House, FDR was elected for an unprecedented fourth term, only to die a few months later, catapulting Harry Truman into the presidency.

The St. Louis Cardinals snatched the World Series from the St. Louis Browns, 4-2. Later that same year, Army beat Navy 23-7, for the first time in five years.

1944 was the year that the Allies liberated Paris, Americans fell in love with Bogart and the Glenn Miller's plane was lost at sea.

It was a year of nationwide patriotism, concern about labor strikes and economic progress.

1944...a year of dramatic change...a year of endurance...a year to remember.

I remember very little for the first three years that we lived in Pastoria, AR. Louise had some interest in one of the Pipkin boys. However, there was an air force retiree, James Delmar (J.D.) Green that seemed more interesting. He would fly over our house at a low altitude just to get her attention. This must have been a great move on his part because it wasn't long before they were married. They moved to Grady, AR and began working on a farm. J.D. (Deck) got a job working for a farm owner. This was a little better than sharecropping because it paid by the month.

Louise and J.D. (Deck) Green

Louis had also gotten married by this time, and our immediate family was a little smaller. He married a girl named, Nadine Varnell, from Kennet, MO. How they met, I'll never know.

Nadine and Louis Frye

Louis also began a career in sharecropping, and later he worked for a landowner by the month. They lived just a couple miles down the road from us. As always, if you worked for a landowner, he would provide you with a house, not much of a house, but a place to call home. You just had to make the best of what you had and like it. Louis and Nadine soon had a son, Charles Edward Frye. He was born in September 1944, and I was born on November 1944. Therefore, the day I was born, I became an uncle to Charles. Then, Louis and his wife had a second son in 1945, Billy Eugene Frye. This made three Frye boys with me as their Uncle Johnny. We grew up together through the hard times. Most of my school friends thought we were brothers and some still today think we were brothers. The next birth in Louis' family was a girl, Rosemary, (Cissi). Later, they would have three more boys, Jimmy (Tinker),

Roger Dale and Danny Lee for a total of six kids. My sister later had only one child, a girl named Barbara Ann Green.

One thing I can say about my family is that we were always a close-knit family. We cared about and loved one another in a very special way. We never showed much outward affection for one another, but we were family. I cannot remember my dad ever saying that he loved me, but I know he must have. I was the baby of the family, and everybody loved the baby. There was never enough money, but we seemed to have the things that we needed to get us by. And for us kids, we didn't know any better, except when we began school we saw what other kids had. Most of them were not as poor as we were. Most of the farmhouses were scattered. As far as I can remember, there were never any neighborhood kids near us. But later, as nephews and a niece came along, there were kids to play with.

Up unto now, I have guessed at the facts along with some that I had been told to relay this story as it unfolded. Now in 1947, I was three years old, and I can remember the real facts of the growth and future of our Frye family. Since I was the last child to be born into our family, and my youngest brother was 9 years older than me, I was always the baby. Therefore, being the loving family that I had been born to, I was treated special. As I grew older, I could not understand this attention. I just wanted to be treated as the other children. My family overprotected me and provided special care for me. I think sometimes they were somewhat jealous of me because I had been born later in life. Therefore, I did not have to go though some of the hard times that they had experienced. Like I said, it was a very hard life, but we were very happy with what we had, and we just made the best of it.

Chapter 3: The Move to the City

Mom, Dad, Johnny and Barbara Green

The commercial fishing must have been really good this
year because we were able to move to the city. Pine Bluff,
AR was the place for our next move. My father purchased
a house and a small fish market on Cedar Street. This fish
market also sold a small amount of dry goods and some
alcohol and beer. My father did whatever he could to
make some money. I remember that he used a straight
razor for shaving. He would offer shaves in the market
area to the patrons for a price. I can remember this razor
deal very well because he had a strap that he used to keep
the razor sharp. This razor strap was used for a threat to
Bill and me to keep us in tow. As far as I know, he never
used it on us. But, I think he got real close on several
occasions.

I can remember a vendor that would come in from Rison, AR and sell my father some wild hog meat, which he would then prepare and sell. He would grind up some of the meat into sausage and cut the rest up in hams and shoulders. I think there were also some of the intestines used for chitterlings. I know there were pickled pig's feet. They were not that bad, if you ate them before the salty vinegar dried off.

We had a garden and a few chickens. Sometimes, for Sunday lunch, there would be some fried chicken; boy was this good. It just took some time and a lot of hard work to get this chicken dinner. Dad or Bill caught the chicken and dressed it for cooking. Mom then fried it up. She could fry chicken with the best of them. I think what made it so good was that she fried it in pure lard.

There had to be a license or permit to sell beer. My father was able to obtain this license, so, as far as I know, we were legal. However, on several occasions he made some of his own beer. This was called "home brew." I don't think this was legal, even though I don't think he ever sold any of it. He only shared it with family and friends. This home brew fermented for several days after it was made. My father looked after this process very closely, and when the time came, there was a great celebration. Times were really rough back then. I think most people of our society drank when they got the opportunity, just for some sort of relief and enjoyment.

We had moved up in the world with our own place of business. But I am still amazed that we were able to have this place. We still had the outhouse deal. However, there was only one, which was shared by the fish market patrons. Therefore, the timing had to be right to get to use it. These places had a very distinctive smell, which was always bad. Also, during the nighttime, we had a little more convenience. There was a pot called the "slop jar" that we used. This pot was stored under the bed and was taken out to do your business in. Then, either you covered it after use and placed it back under the bed; or if the smell was too bad, it had to be taken outside and dumped. This was particularly helpful during the cold winter months. Sounds rather horrible, but it worked.

Sometimes I was allowed to visit the fish market, which was adjacent to our house. They would not allow me to go in there much because they sold and drank a lot of beer in there. Dad had a special beer vendor that came into the market, and on each visit he wanted to see me. He sold Pabst Blue Ribbon beer. Once he gave me a small rabbit savings bank. He thought this was a very special rabbit to me, and each time he visited the fish market, he gave me a nickel and a soda pop, and he would watch me put the nickel into the rabbit bank. I saved several nickels. However I never knew what became of it. I guess my parents must have taken this money to buy me something special. After all, I was the baby of the family and everyone treated me special.

I can remember one time for Christmas I got a red wagon. I rode in this wagon for hours and pretended it was my truck. I sat in the back of it with my legs over the sides and pushed it forever. I could push backwards better than forwards and got pretty good at getting around in it. Sometimes I hauled some articles from the house to the fish market. Everyone seemed impressed that I used this wagon in this fashion. I also liked to ride in it if I could get anyone to pull me around. I don't remember this happening very much.

We seemed to have more than we ever had in our lives. Our house was not much to look at, but it was just as good as any in the neighborhood. In 1948, the racial issue was around loud and clear. I had to learn a lot about this as I grew older. I could not understand the way this separation was handled during these years. Our new place was right in the middle of a colored neighborhood, and we had many colored customers. I didn't have any concern about this, but as I grew older, I began to see the different ways people were treated. There were many places in town that served both colored and white; however, the white people were served on one side of the place and the colored on the other side. Restrooms were the same way. There was one for the white and one for the colored. I do not think that my father ever separated the two at his fish market. This practice, I am sure must not have pleased everyone. However, I can't remember any trouble coming from this issue. We treated everyone the same, and some of our closest friends were colored.

We had a storm cellar. It was a concrete pit constructed with logs on top and covered with sod and a wooden door. It was located out in our yard. There were several tornados or as many called them back then, "cyclones." There were many of these in this area during the springtime. Many times, we had to use this cellar for protection. Most of the time, when we got in there our next-door neighbor would already be there. It smelled musky and damp, for it leaked. The walls and ceiling were mildewed and looked terrible. I hated to go in there.

There was a ground well for household water. I thought this was neat. It was about four feet across, with a shed over the top. A long tin dipper was lowered down into the well by an attached rope. The dipper filled with water and a flap closed and held it in place until the dipper was pulled back up. Then water was drained into a container for drinking, washing clothes, bathing, etc. The drinking water was poured into a water bucket and placed on a counter in the kitchen. There was a metal dipper that was hung on the side of the bucket. Everyone - visitors, friends, and family drank from this dipper and placed it back into the water bucket for the next person to use. Yuck!!!

There was no washing machine. My mother had a large black pot that she would use to boil water to wash our clothes. She would soak the clothes in this boiling water and stir them with a wooden paddle. Then, she would take them out and rub them over a board. This was an apparatus called a "rub board." It is about 12"x 24" with short legs. It was mostly covered with corrugated tin. She used this rub board to rub all of the dirty spots out of our clothes. She would rinse them in some cold water and then squeeze the water out of them. Then the clothes were hung on an outside clothesline to air-dry. On special occasions, she had a couple of irons that she would heat and press our clothes with.

We were moving on up. We had a nice house, and we had some of the conveniences that we had never had before, such as furniture. We had only one bedroom. Everyone slept in the same room. I remember we had two iron bed frames with some sort of mattresses and quilts that my mother had made by hand. One thing I can remember that she always like to sew, especially quilts. She would take old scrapes of cloth and sew them together for the quilt tops. Flour sacks were real popular back then. She would take these sacks when they were emptied and cut them into square pieces of cloth and sew them together. Also, with the purchase of these sacks of flour, we would get a small washcloth. I think this started as a promotion just to get everyone to buy a certain kind of flour.

We also, had obtained a radio. Every Saturday night, we all gathered around this radio and listened to the Grand Ole Opry. Shelby Lewis and Sarah Jane were local country and western singers that we listened to often. My father had a violin (fiddle) and could play it very well. I still have that violin and case. It is not in good enough shape to use or sell. I would like to have it restored someday. Bill had a guitar, and he could play it very well. I don't know how he learned to play. Dad must have taught him. Bill could not read music. He played by ear. If he heard a tune, he could play it. I remember he and dad would play music together on occasion. They were pretty good.

The cooking took place on a kerosene cook stove. It was called a "coal oil" stove for some reason. Mother cooked some very good meals on this stove for many years. We kind of got used to the coal oil smell and taste after a while. We all bathed in a number 3 washtub. Therefore, we didn't bathe very frequently. Mother would heat the water, and then most of us would bathe in the same water. That is, If we were not too dirty.

We also bought an old Dodge pickup truck that would barely run. We only used this on rare occasions. After all, it ran on gas, and we didn't have extra money for gas or oil. It probably used about as much oil as it did gas. For heat in the winter, we had a wood stove that kept us warm on one side, and then we could turn to the other side. This was used only during our waking hours. At bedtime, the stove was allowed to cool off. And I mean, some nights it cooled off really well. I can remember some nights when it would get really cold, Mother would heat the irons that she used to press our clothes and place them under our quilts at the foot of the bed. This was a real comfort, even though they didn't stay hot very long. Most of the times we would go to sleep before the irons got really cool. The first one up in the morning would start the fire in our wood stove. We would split some small wood into kindling so that we could start the fire easily. I was too young for this process to include me; therefore, I would stay in bed until I could feel the warmth. I think this may be the first bad habit that I learned. Let someone else do the hard work, and then reap the benefits. But that was never me. I have always liked hard work and never step away from it.

Back then, everyone, even on the farm, would work six days a week. No one worked on Sunday. Even all of the stores in the city were closed, and many would attend church, although my family never attended.

Exodus 20:8

Remember the Sabbath day, to keep it holy.

Momma was the only one that would say anything about God or church. Every Sunday, the neighbors right on the next street behind us, would come home from church and have an outside singing. I think it may have been their church choir practicing or something because there were a lot of people singing church hymns. I remember they were very loud. Everyone around could hear this singing. It was good for a little while, and then it would start to bother you. I guess no one ever complained because they just kept singing up into the night.

I can remember one night we received a telegram from Maryland that told us one of mother's brothers, Calvin Wenner, had died. This was my first encounter with death. Mother was very sad; however, no way were we able to go to Maryland for the funeral. Later in life, I would get to meet his son and family. That is a very precious family to me. We would visit back and forth on several occasions, but that would be several years from now. As you could say, there would be a lot of water pass under the bridge before this would happen.

Mother would get letters and pictures frequently from her sisters back in Maryland. She never returned to see them. I have wished several times that I would have been in a position to take her back there for a visit and let her tell me her story of growing up from a little girl. I know this would have been very interesting. She passed away before I was financially able to afford this trip for her.

Charles (Buddy), my next to the oldest brother and my youngest brother, Bill, attended Dollarway Public School for a while. Buddy met a young lady, Laverne. She was very beautiful. She was the daughter of some friends of the family. Buddy decided to quit school and get a job so that they could get married. He did just that. He got a job driving a Goldcrest 51 Beer Truck, delivering beer. It was not long after he got this job that he and this beautiful young lady were married. They moved to an upstairs apartment on Main Street in Pine Bluff, AR. This was only a few miles from our house, so we were able to visit often.

That left me and my youngest brother the only kids at home. Since the old Dodge truck didn't run very well, most of the time, we had to travel by foot or ride on what they called a street bus. This bus ride was not free, but it cost only a few cents. I remember my mother and I would take the street bus grocery shopping to the downtown Safeway. We would only have $5 to spend. You would be surprised what $5 would purchase in 1948. As any young boy would do, I would find several things in the grocery store that I wanted to take home with me. At that time, I could not understand why we could not afford these things. My mother would take me by the hand and pull me along. I don't know what had happened to her right thumb; but it had been operated on for some sort of bone issue. She called it a bone felon, whatever that may be. But when she would sink that thumb into me, I sure knew she meant business.

In 1950:

- A car cost $1550
- Gasoline was $0.26/gal.
- A new house cost $13,500
- A loaf of bread cost $0.14
- Milk cost $0.86/gal.
- A postage stamp cost $0.03
- The stock market was at 177
- The average annual salary was $3,600
- The unemployment rate was 5.4%

- The minimum wage was $0.40/hr.

I remember, Bill would come home from school and play some pass football with one of the neighbor kids. This was ok with my mother. However, there was a team that practiced football near our home, and we were not allowed to go watch this action. My mother said that this game was too dangerous, and people could be killed in this sport. Players grabbed each other and threw them to the ground with much authority. No way were we to have anything to do with this or even watch others. Bill was very stoutly built, and you could see his biceps growing. Not me, I never was very big. I was skinny as a rail and stayed that way until I got married several years later. I weighed only 130 pounds when I graduated high school and was 5'11" tall. I have now shrunk to 5'10" tall and weigh 190 pounds. I have a good wife with good cooking.

Good times availed for a couple of years. Continuation of this free enterprise system would have been a **"Turn in Life"** experience for me. When I grew older, I could have moved right into the fish market or grocery business if we had been more successful with this process. I have thought a lot about getting into some sort of business; however, the opportunity or money never really came. I got real close a few times to venturing out on my own. I would have to risk everything. I have never been willing to do this, since I had started with nothing and certainly got no inheritance.

Over the years, I have seen many many people get a great start on life by having families that had already made it financially in life, and all these lucky people had to do was to maintain and grow the family business or farm the inherited farmland. This must have been a real blessing for some kids. However, I am sure this type of living was not easy either, for I have also seen many people not willing to put in the difficult effort to maintain or move forward. So they would either lose their inheritance or sell out. Then, most would be broke within a few years.

As fate would have it, times became more and more difficult. Business in the fish market took a turn for the worse. Customers became less and less frequent, and the ones who showed up had very little or no money. Most of them now wanted credit. My dad started running a tab for the people that he thought would pay. Times were really bad, and even these people could not pay, for they had nothing. Some bartering took place. Dad accepted a mid-size pendulum clock, and my mother really liked it. This thing was a nuisance. It struck a dong at every number of the hour, and once on the half hour. After a while, I think we got used to it. I must have because I lived with this thing for the next forty years or so. I still have it today in the attic storage. We had also gotten a Victorola record player. This played the 33 1/3 rpm-records as well as the smaller 45s. It had to be cranked before playing; the more you cranked, the longer it played.

Eventually, my father had to approach the bank. There was no money for the mortgage payment. After a very few months, he had to call it quits. I was not old enough to understand what was happening. This certainly was a **"Turn in Life"** experience that was about to happen to my entire family. My father acquired $1200 from the equity of the property. We had to leave soon. No one knew what was to come now.

My family began to talk of a young colored girl that visited the fish market on a regular basis. They said that my dad had become very friendly toward her. The next thing I knew, my dad said he would head to California and seek out a new life for us. When he got things set up, he would have us come out there.

In the mean time, we were to live with my older brother, Louis and his family. He now had three kids and a fourth on the way. That would be no problem, for we were very good at just making do with whatever the situation warranted. My mother always thought that my father ran off with this young colored girl. If so, no one ever found out. Therefore, we moved in with Louis, and we didn't hear anything from my father for almost a year. My youngest brother, Bill, quit school and began to help Louis on the farm. He worked by the day for the landowner and received a very small wage.

We didn't have much stuff to move but we still had to get rid of some things. We could only keep the essentials. Like the beds and the coal oil cook stove. I remember there were no way that we could keep the Victorola and the many records that we had accumulated. Bill and I had fun tossing these records out across the neighborhood like Frisbees, which we had never heard of. Maybe this could have been a real life invention for us. However, even though we had not heard of the Frisbee, it had been around for a while. Some records show that it was invented in 1938. The Frisbie Baking Company sold pies in tins that, when emptied, could be tossed and caught easily, and from there many people could be found tossing things in the air like Frisbees. This would provide many hours of fun and sport. Today the toy maker giant, Mattel, owns the Frisbee. I think we could have sold some of the records to others for Frisbee throwing, if they could have known how much fun we were having. Oh. I forgot most people were broke almost as much as we were. But, I wish I had boxed those records and saved that old Victorola. They may be worth something today. I think it was already an antique.

Chapter 4: The Unbelievable Years

This was in 1951, and I was turning seven years old. We were still living with Louis and his family. I thought nothing about this at the time, but there was quite a crowd in their one bedroom house. By this time, Louis and Nadine had two boys, Charles and Billy, and one girl, Rosemary (Cissi). One thing I can remember, Nadine would make chocolate gravy and biscuits every morning for breakfast. This was good, but every morning? Every once in a while, she would break the routine, and we had regular gravy and biscuits.

Now I was school age. My birthday was in November, so I didn't begin school until I was nearly seven years old. Charles, "Bulb," as he was called, had already started to school at Sherrill Barrett School. Back then, there was no kindergarten, we just went right to the first grade. He didn't know anyone there and didn't know how to act around strangers. This was a bad year for Bulb. Later, I could certainly relate to this. Anyway, he was held back, and he had to repeat the first grade, which was a blessing in disguise because his younger brother, Billy and I started to school the next year. That put us all three in the same grade. Now that was a pretty picture. We were fine with this set up. We played together and made some friends. We played cowboys and Indians with our stick guns, and we ran, ran, and ran. In our school, there were a couple of tall slides, a couple of merry-go-rounds, and a set of monkey bars. I think I still have some of the calluses on the palms of my hands from hanging from those monkey bars.

Many of the kids were good at this. Some of them could go from end to end by skipping every other bar. I don't think I ever accomplished this task, but I tried many times. One of the two slides on the playground had a curved chute, and this was a real challenge; however, most of us got this done, even though it was a little scary at first.

As we were playing during recess one day, we found some tall grass that had some cattails in it. Some of us boys had tried this before; therefore, we were experienced. We told Jimmy Fowler, one of our classmates, that we dared him to place a small piece of the cattail under his tongue. He said he could do it. So, here we go. He placed it there; of course, that was not the problem. You could get it under the tongue fairly easy, but you could not get it out because some of the bristles would get lodged when you tried to remove it. The more you tried to move it; the deeper it would get under your tongue. Jimmy panicked, and the race was on. He ran to the teacher, and she told him to stick his tongue out as far as he could. Then she took her finger and dug out the piece of cattail. Now this was a sight. We thought for sure we were in a lot of trouble. But, the teacher only told Jimmy to never try this again. I don't think she had to say this, for Jimmy had learned his lesson. He was kind of mad at us for a while, but he got over it.

One chore that I can remember from the first grade was learning to count. Mrs. Rachel Mitchell, our teacher, had a bag of acorns that we used for counting. This was difficult, but fun. I was learning something. I learned to read a little in the first grade. *Fun with Dick and Jane* was a very popular reading book then. I never really had been taught much at home about what I should expect at school. I had begun to pattern myself after some of the things that my brothers and sister were doing. **I think that this is a very good point**. We become who we associate with, without ever being mindful of our actions, if we are not careful. This being said, I think it is very important who we become friends with or who we allow our children to become associated with. I have always tried to be around someone who could offer me some guidance in my growth in life. Remember, my glass is always half full.

This was another very tough year. My sister and her husband, J.D., got Bill a job on the farm that J.D. was overseeing in Grady, AR. That was great, but this meant that we had to move to Grady. We moved into a vacant house near my sister. I did not understand what an impact this would have on me, having to change school in the middle of first grade. I was not ready to leave my two nephews and my other first grade friends.

This was going to be quite an experience for me. I did not have a clue how to make this transition. I really didn't know how to make new friends. Since this move happened in the middle of my first year of school, the new class that I attended had already gotten set in the way that they did things, and it was nothing like the Sherrill Barrett School. I hated it from the beginning, but I tried to make the best of it.

I remember taking a spelling test. At the Sherrill School, we only had small easy words. The teacher would give us the words in advance so that we could study them. This made it very easy to get most of them correct. However, the Grady School was a little different. The first grade teacher would give us the words to study, all right. But during the test, she would state the word, and before I could even begin to spell it, she would use it in a sentence. Now, this was so confusing for me, for I would try to spell every word in the sentence and write it down. After all, this was a spelling test, and for some reason, I thought that I had to spell everything she said during the test. What a mess my paper must have been. I could spell the words that I had studied; but I bet the teacher had a lot of trouble finding these words in my jumbled up mess of a test paper. She never said anything to me about this.

I had to walk out to the end of our dirt road from the house to the main gravel road to catch the school bus. This was about a quarter of a mile. This was quite a challenge during the winter months. When the weather got really bad, I would get to stay home. Wow, I liked these days. But, this would get me farther behind in class and make my first grade even more difficult. I did make some friends; however, they were no Bulb and Billy and the Sherrill gang. I was very home sick, but this was my new home. What was I to do?

Times were still very tough at home. Bill worked most every day when it was not raining, and he brought home a small paycheck. But remember, we had nothing but some of the furniture that was left from the Pine Bluff move. Daddy had taken all of the money with him. We had a small garden for fresh vegetables. Most of the meals were beans and potatoes and mostly beans. There was a poke salad patch nearby, and in season we would have some poke salad greens. These were a little like turnip greens, only they tasted just a little more bitter. These were a good change, sometimes.

Louise and (Deck), as J.D. was called, would have us over occasionally. I remember Deck liked sliced, pressed ham. Boy, was this good! There was not much of it, and it was sliced real thin, but I could have one piece. I would savor this and eat it real slow for the lasting enjoyment.

Deck had a shed where the tractors were stored and repaired. On rainy days, Bill and Deck would throw washers into a hole for a game. This looked like fun. I would help them retrieve the washers when they went astray. If I was to have any fun, I had to make my own fun out of whatever I could. Barbara Ann and I played together some, but I was not into playing with the things girls liked at this time. So I just hung around with the adults when I could. I loved to go to the field with them. I would carry them water when they needed it. Later, when we had family and laborers chop the weeds from our cotton fields, I would be the water boy. I can hear them calling now "Water Boy"! I would carry a bucket of cold water out to them in the field. Again, there was only one dipper.

Everyone drank from this dipper. No one thought anything of this. Everyone just did it. They seemed like they would call me when they got to the far end of the row. And boy, were those rows long. It didn't take me long to wise up to this. When they would get near my end of the row, I would serve them water whether they needed it or not.

Chapter 5: The Father Returns

After almost a year had gone by, Mother said she had received a letter from my daddy. All the time he had been gone, there was very little mention of him around me. I missed him at first, but I made do. He hadn't had much to do with me when he was around. Anyway, I heard my mother say that he had spent all of the $1200, and he wanted to come home. I don't know anything about this decision, but I think my mother based the decision on Louise and me. I think she wanted me to have a father in the home.

I can still see my father coming up the dirt road that I walked to catch my school bus everyday. He hugged me at the time, but it was not a large homecoming. My sister got a little emotional, but that was about it. Life began again, just as nothing had happened.

My father fished some of the lakes around Grady. The Arkansas River was only a short distance away. The best fishing was in the floodwater lakes. In the springtime, the river would rise and flood over into the lakes and restock them with river fish. These floodwater lakes were called "bar pits". During a certain time of the year, right after the flooded river had receded from these pits, the fishing was pretty good. However, it was not nearly as good as fishing in the lakes near Pastoria or Pipkin Lake. One day, I remember my dad took me to one of the bar pits to check his trotlines. I had to stay on the shore and watch. I saw him having a really rough time landing some of the large fish. He caught a couple of large catfish. One was a river catfish that weighed about 30 pounds, and the other was a flathead catfish that weighed just as much. These would have been some excellent eating. But, no, these had to be sold. The flathead, or "Appaloosa Cat" as they were called, is very good eating. They have a very big, flat head and feed on live bait. The head is just about as large as the body. They have a soft white meat and are really tasty, whereas the river catfish is a scavenger. He feeds on the bottom and eats everything that gets in his way.

The bar pits were really good for swimming. A very sad note I can remember is a family up the way from us had lost a daughter. She had drowned in one of these bar pits. She had attempted to swim across one of these pits and didn't make it. This was my second recognition of death.

I could not understand how God could allow this to happen, especially to someone this young. Later, I learned the verse from

Romans 8:28

And we know that all things work together for good to them that love God, to them who are called according to his purpose.

This would become my favorite verse in the Bible. I found I could hold onto this verse no matter what happened. With this verse in my heart, I could know that God was still in control.

God is omnipresent, and he is omniscient and omnipotent. He is everywhere and knows everything, and He is all-powerful.

He knows all of the decisions that we will make in our lives, even before we make them, even though he still allows us to make our own decisions. That may be difficult to understand, but remember:

Luke 22:34

And he said, I tell thee, Peter,the cock, shall not crow this day, before that thou shalt thrice deny that thou knowest me.

Peter said that this would never happen. But he denied Jesus three times just as Jesus had said. Now we need to understand that Jesus did not make this decision for Peter. It was Peter's decision at the time, and Jesus knew in advance the decision that Peter would make. Just as he knows what all of our decisions will be in our life before we make them, but we still have the choice to make them ourselves. This is just a little confusing for non-believers, but by faith we have God, and He is still in control. He knows everything, He is everywhere, and He is all-powerful. But be aware, Satan also has very much power, just not as much power as Jesus. He has the power to make the worse things seem like fun.

From some of the money Dad had made from selling fish, he bought an old "T" Model car. Boy, was it ugly. It looked like one of those old gangster cars that you now see in old movies. It had a starter on it, but there was no battery. There was a crank right in front of it by the front bumper. It was pretty difficult to turn, but the "T" Model would start after several cranks. Dad finally got smart about this cranking thing. We lived right by a high river levee. When he came home, he would park this car on top of the levee, and when he got ready to go somewhere, we would push it down the levee with it in gear, and it would start. That is, most of the time.

Now, as the sharecropping progressed, times were still very hard. The somewhat good times that we had enjoyed in Pine Bluff were gone. We were nearly back to where we began. I can remember only one real argument that my mother and dad had. It was when Dad told Mother that she was spending too much on food. I don't know what this was all about because I didn't see much food, just the same old beans and potatoes, and mostly beans. This argument got really heated, but everyone at least stayed together.

Between the sharecrop salary and what dad made as a commercial fisherman, we were able to survive awhile longer. School was getting tougher by the day for me just to attend. I woke up early one morning and decided that I was not going to school. My mother thought differently. She told me "yes" I was going to school. I decided to test her. She got out the fine switch that I had gotten accustomed to and let me have it. Before I knew it, I had taken my medicine. I was still stinging; however, I was pretty sure she was finished with me, and I had survived, so why should I change my mind now? So, I said that I still was not going to school. She said the switch was still ready to go again. Then she said something that I didn't want to hear. She said she would tell Earl; this is what she called my dad. Well, she told Earl, and he got out the razor strap. Now, there was no way I was going to let this happen. But, I had made up my mind that I was not going to school. After all, I thought that I had gone through enough punishment to win this argument. Therefore, I ran fast enough that my dad could not catch me. I thought that I had really crossed the line this time. After chasing me around the farm equipment for a while, he gave up and said that he would deal with me when I came home for bed. Now, this wasn't fair. What was I to do because it was too late to catch the school bus?

Well, this is what happened. My father must have had other very important things on his mind besides me because he never whipped me for this. But you bet your bottom dollar that I didn't try this again. The next day, I got up early to attend school. I still didn't like it, but I was going to make the best of it. Also, my mother had warned me that if I didn't attend school, my bus driver, who was on the board of the "Boys Reform School", would come and take me away because there was a law that I had to attend school. It didn't make any difference whether I liked it or not.

This could have been a **"Turn in Life"** if my parents had not cared enough for me to make me stay in school. My other brothers and sister were allowed to quit school at an early age, but certainly not this early in their school years. They could at least read and write.

I think, looking back, everyone was determined to make sure that I would have a better life than they had lived. But this better life was still many years away. But, I will be forever grateful for my family and their loving care for me. We were a family and could make the best of a bad situation. And yes, I did finish the first grade, and somehow, I passed on to the second grade.

Now, more bad news was coming to us. After the crop was harvested, there was no money owed to us. Our money allowance had barely matched the total pay for our share of the crop. This was very disappointing. We didn't know what to do now. Even though my father had been fishing some of the river lakes near Grady, at this time of the year, the bar pits were not very good at producing any fish. It would be next spring before the river would flood over into these lakes and restock them. There would be no income for several months or until the next year, when another crop could be planted.

The only good thing here was that we had no bills, and we had each other. And remember, I was still the baby of the family; therefore, they would treat me as if we had everything. My family would do without so that I could have the best, which wasn't very good, but I didn't know any better.

Chapter 6: Back to Pastoria

My family began to look for options. Since Louis was sort of in a stable situation with his job, he inquired around for a job for us. He found us one. Harvey Braden was looking for some help. His farm was on the Pipkin Plantation. This was near where we had lived before.

God must have been looking over us. For God knew what we needed at this time. Even though we were not Christians, I know that God still loved us. I certainly was not old enough to understand this, but looking back, I know that God knows everything. I had to go through these trials with my family in order to get to my place in life. God will not allow us to have more trouble than we can bear. He is always there for us. Remember, he is everywhere. That means he is always with us, through the good times and the bad times. Just trust him.

Bill went to visit Mr. Braden, and everything was all set to begin to work ASAP. My dad also liked this move because it would put him back near Pipkin Lake where we had started. This was a good lake for a commercial fisherman, and he thought he could make a lot of money fishing this lake, just as he had once done.

So, here we go. Mr. Braden borrowed a bob truck for us to use. He had a house near his farm that was vacant, and he said we could live there while we were working for him.

I guess I was excited, at least until we drove up to the house. He was right; no one had lived in this house for some time. It was about a ¼ mile off the main gravel road, and we couldn't even see it until we drove the bob truck right up near the porch. The hogweeds were nearly as tall as the house.

But, this was to be home for now. Bill and Louis unloaded the truck with our stuff, which wasn't much because we had gotten rid of most of our possessions during the move from Pine Bluff. Here we were, ready to start anew again. No water, no outhouse, just us.

We had to carry our water from Mr. Braden's farmhouse. It was about 500 yards away. The next thing we had to do was dig a hole for the outhouse. This was not too difficult. You would just dig a hole and construct some sort of box unit over it, just to give you some privacy while you did your job.

There was one good thing with this situation; it was about time for me to begin school. I would be in the second grade, and I would be there with Bulb and Billy. Just as I did in Grady, I would walk down to the end of the dirt road and catch the school bus to Sherrill Barrett School.

School was now cool. I was learning to read and write a little. We all had an art bag. This was a cloth bag with a pull string. It contained our scissors, paste, crayons, etc. Mrs. Dorothy Bell was my second grade teacher. It was her first year of teaching. She was young and very nice. She was very high on good hygiene. At the start of each class day, she would have us go through a hygiene checklist. Did we wash our face, did we brush our teeth, etc.? This was easy for most of the kids. However, I had to step it up a little to pass this checklist. Of course, the No. 3 washtub was still around, so I could clean up a bit. However, there was no toothpaste. My mother told me that she had some baking soda that would work just fine. I used this every day, and some days I would pass this checklist, when they didn't check real close. They would ask us if we brushed our teeth. Of course, I could say yes without any explanation and try to look very truthful. But, when they would actually check closely, I didn't fare so well.

I really liked the Sherrill School and all of the teachers. I would not trade this experience for anything. It played a major part of my growing up. God was always there for me, and he knew what I needed and when I needed it. We didn't have much, but we were family.

The Sherrill School did not teach us much about organization. When school would let out at the end of the day, there would be a mass exit for the front door. The first grade was allowed to get out of class a couple of minutes before the end of school bell rang. But the rest of the classes were on their own. When it was time for this bell to ring everyone would be on the edge of their seats, waiting to run out into the hall and out those front doors. Everyone would race to see who could get out first and onto the waiting buses. There would be a lot of pushing and shoving going on for a couple of minutes. This was a sight to see for sure.

School was going fine. I was learning a little bit. Mrs. Denison was our 3rd grade teacher. I remember that we were studying math, and I had done real well with the addition part. Now we were into subtraction. It gave me a few more problems for a while. One day, Mrs. Denison gave us an exam on subtraction. I had addition on my mind, and I missed all of the problems. She gave me a D for some reason. This was the worst grade that I had ever gotten. Since this was only one test, I was able to get this grade up to a B by the time our report cards came out. I think this taught me a lesson in life. Pay a little more attention to the instructions.

We stayed here at Harvey Braden's Farm for a couple of years and barely got by. Then we moved to a couple more farms in the area, and Bill worked by the day, and Daddy would still catch fish to sell.

By the time I was 10 years old and in the fourth grade, another major event took place in my life. I was now allowed to go fishing with by dad and help him. He had a wooden v-hull fishing boat. There was no motor for this boat, just oars and paddles. We would go out on the lake to check Dad's trotlines. Each time we had to paddle about ½ mile and back. I helped with the paddling, if I could do it correctly. You had to pull with the paddle, and right before you finished the pull, you would have to flip the paddle one way or the other, depending on the way you wanted to steer the boat. In the beginning, I could only paddle in a straight line, and Dad did all of the steering. I can still hear my father yelling that I had my paddle turned in the wrong direction. This made it more difficult for him to row the boat. You have to live and learn, and I learned pretty quickly under these circumstances.

Sometimes, I would get real tired and wanted to go home early. I was allowed to take this walk home alone. I can remember I hated to walk along the floodgate ditch that led out to the gravel road. There were many snakes in this ditch. It seemed as though they were on every tree limb that extended down into the water. Sometimes they would be lying in the pathway. Before I left the campsite, Dad would tell me to be careful. I was scared, and sometimes I would run real fast by the snakes. I guess I thought that they couldn't bite me if I ran fast enough. I was not thinking that if had I stepped on one, he would have bitten me for sure. On the way home along the ditch of the gravel road, there were many snakes called "blue racers". My dad said these snakes liked to chase you. None ever chased me, but I could hear them moving through the grass along the ditch, or maybe this was my imagination. I never took a chance and tried to find one of these snakes. I certainly didn't want to get acquainted with one of them.

There was a flood levee near the main gravel road that I used to walk home. If I could make it to that levee, I felt pretty safe from the snakes. When I got to the top of the levee, there it was; I could see the house at the "Blue Hole" where I was born. Boy, many times I wished that we still lived there because if we did, I would now be home and not have to make this two-mile walk. Sometimes as I was walking, there would be a friend who came along in a vehicle and gave me a ride. This was a blessing when it happened, although there was not much traffic during this era. Not too many people had vehicles.

Along the road home, there lived a couple of farmers who had about 10 acres of land. They always grew cotton on the land, and they also had a huge garden beside the road that we traveled. These were two brothers, and they were huge and tough looking men. They lived on this farm alone; neither had a wife. Dad said they were from Sweden. Their names were Elijah and Elisha. All of us kids were always afraid of them. They were quiet and never talked with anyone. They may not have been able to speak much English. They didn't have a tractor to work their farm. They had a pair of old mules and two oxen. I thought this was kind of strange, since no one else farmed this way.

I guess they knew what they were doing because they would always have the first bale of cotton to the gin each year. I think they were given a prize for this. They worked really hard to make this happen each year.

During these years, my dad taught me a lot about fishing and hunting. I still like to fish very much today. I hunted quite a bit in my younger years, but I haven't hunted in a while. I will have a few hunting stories later in my next book, especially duck hunting. I enjoyed this hunting the best.

My father and I did some sport fishing; however, you had to be very careful, since we were commercial fishermen. You could not do any sport fishing if you had any commercial fishing equipment in your possession. I think we were legal most of the time. Anyway, I remember a certain treetop near a far bank in the Pipkin Lake where we caught a few nice crappies. These were the best fish for eating. We would just scale them and clean them for frying. We cooked them whole, no fileting at this time. We just had to be careful to watch out for the small bones.

One morning after checking all of our commercial lines, we went to our campsite and unloaded all of our commercial equipment, and away we went to this crappie hole. Before we could go out, we had to unload all of our catch for the morning. We placed these fish into a fish box or net that was located just out from the shore, near our fish camp. This was made of a wire mesh with a wooden door on it to keep it afloat. A fish market owner came by a couple of times a week to buy our catch. To me, this was fun, but to my family, it brought in just enough money to buy more fishing equipment and have a little left over for food.

When we arrived at our crappie hole, we found that the crappie were not too hungry that day. We only caught a few, but they were good ones. Of course, dad caught the most. I don't think I caught any on this trip. Now we had to paddle, paddle, and paddle back to shore. Dad said that he wanted to try another spot that he thought might hold some crappie. When we arrived, I hurriedly baited my hook with a good live minnow and dropped it into a good spot. Low and behold, my cork didn't even stop when it hit the water. Now the fight was on! The fish was pulling just as hard as I was. I finally won the battle and got him on board. It was a drum. Or some called these fish "Sheep head" or "Gaspergoos". I was going to toss this fish back into the water, and Dad said he knew of someone who really liked to eat this kind of fish. They would probably buy it from me. That sounded very good.

These people lived about a mile from our fishing campsite. This would be about half way home. Dad and I would walk about two miles each day from our home to our Pipkin Lake campsite. Since Dad stayed at the campsite to check our fishing lines again just before dark, I was to take this drum fish on the road for my first sell. Sure enough, these people were glad to get this fish. They wanted to know my price, and I said 50 cents. All they could scrape up was 38 cents. I took this and made my first fish sell. I was so proud of this. I could not wait to tell my dad about this when he got home. He told me not to get too excited because life was difficult, and I had a lot to learn. How true this proved to be as I grew up.

Dad prepared his snag lines on the riverbank. Then he would place the hooks onto a metal rod and snap them into a wooden holder or rack. This was not very complicated but was sort of a delicate process to take these lines to the lake and place them in areas that would produce the most fish. Sometimes we placed these snag lines in a shallow part of the lake, and then we would take our boat paddle and make noise on the side of the boat to scare the fish into our snag line. This was kind of neat. It was a kind of fish round up rodeo.

Dad would tie one end of the snagged line to a wooden pole that he would stick into the bottom of the lake. Then, here is the tricky part, he would have me to slowly paddle the boat out away from this pole to attach the other end of the snag line to another pole that he had placed about 30 or 40 yards away. I remember this very clearly. I had to go slowly at just the correct speed. I also had to negotiate the wind rate into this. This was kind of complicated for me at age 10. I got yelled at more than once. "Hold that boat straight, boy" my dad would yell out.

I think I did pretty well at this most of the time. I remember on one occasion, my dad had me to hold one of the snag lines while he made a hook adjustment. Guess what? I let it slip out of my hands, and it landed in the bottom of the lake. Boy, I thought that would be the end of me. And it nearly was. I don't think my dad ever got over this. We fished this line off the bottom of the lake;

however, with all of these hooks on this line, it was a tangled mess.

Louis and Bill liked to fish a little bit also. They had another idea on how to catch the river fish or the Blue Channel Catfish, which was the best kind of catfish for eating other than the flathead. These flathead fish were not very numerous. Bill and Louis liked to go to the Arkansas River and fish from the riverbank. They had a very interesting way to catch these Channel catfish. They used what they called a throw line. This was a heavy main line that had 10 hooks trailing off of it for about 15 inches. They would bait these hooks with what we called buck shot worms. These worms were large and tough, and they would remain on the hook in the swift river current. They tied one end of the main line to a stake placed in the ground near the water line in a very swift area of the river. This seemed to be the best place to catch these channel cats. They would line the hooks up on the bank and then tie a large river rock on the other end of it. Then they would bait the 10 hooks with the buckshot worms and throw it out into the river until the line would become tight from the stake.

They would have several lines of this nature in a long stretch along the shoreline. These lines would remain untouched until early the next morning. Then they went to each stake and pulled in the lines with several fish on the hooks. This was considered sport fishing. They would have great fish for us to eat, and they would also sell several of them for some much needed money.

Sometimes Bill and I took our rods and reels and fished in the river. One day, Bill hooked onto a giant blue catfish. It weighed 20 pounds. We were fishing with 12-pound test line, so we had to be careful landing this fish. When Bill got the fish pulled near the shore, which was really rocky, he thought these rocks might break his line, so he handed me the rod and told me to hold on very tight. Then he went right into the river, clothes and all. He wrestled with this catfish until he got him on shore. This kind of scared me at first, and then I saw that Bill had everything under control. Boy, did we have some good fried catfish that night for supper.

Sometimes in the early spring, right after the Arkansas River had flooded the entire bar pits, we could catch all of the German carp that we wanted. We caught them by using dough balls for bait. These fish were a little different from most fish. They didn't bite the bait as other fish would. They would suck the bait. Therefore the dough ball worked well. We used a cane fishing pole with a line, hook, sinker, and cork. Most of the time, when these carp began to suck on the dough ball, the cork would not go under; it would just turn up on its side. We would let this action go on for a few seconds, so they could suck in the bait. Then we would set the hook in the jaw of these German carp. Then the action would be on! Sometimes they would pull so hard that they would break our cane poles. This really was a lot of fun.

Most of these carp were be fairly large. They weighted 6-8 pounds. They were not very good; however, we ate them sometimes for the lack of anything else. We only ate the larger ones. The smaller carp had too many tiny bones, and they were hard to eat without getting a bone stuck in your throat. Also, if we caught them from muddy water, they would have a strong or a muddy taste.

In the fall and winter months, there would be no fishing time. My dad did some hunting and trapping. He called it steel trapping, since the traps that he used were made of steel and resembled a bear trap, only a smaller version. He placed these traps in a real condensed area, and then when some wild animal would come by and step in this trap, it would snap shut and trap the animal by the leg. Sometimes dad placed some bait in these traps, and when the animal would take a bite, the trap would catch him by the neck.

Most of the catches were possums, raccoons, and rabbits. We were hoping for a mink or two, since the mink's hides' were worth a lot more than any of the other animals. I don't remember ever catching a mink, even though there were some in the area. Dad would skin these animals very carefully and take the hide and stretch it over an oval shaped board. After they dried, he would sell them in the market.

Most of the time, we ate the meat from these skinned animals. It wasn't too bad, especially the raccoons and rabbits. The possum was the worst thing I ever tried. I think the smell of the oil from the possum cooking turned my stomach. Fried rabbit was the best.

Dad killed a few squirrels, and they were fine eating. Dad would let me go hunting with him from time to time. Just behind our house was a small forest with several large acorn trees. Dad and I still-hunted these squirrels. We would sit down near these acorn trees in the late afternoon. When the squirrels came to feed, we would shoot a few. My dad had a 20 gauge Haven bolt action shot gun. I still have this gun, and it is still in working condition.

We had a couple of old stray dogs that dad had taught to chase rabbits. We took these dogs to the woods, and when they would pick up a rabbit's scent, the action would be on. Dad taught me how to shoot that old 20 gauge. Then, one day he said, "Son, take this gun, and when the dogs turns the rabbit, he will come right by us. Then you shoot the rabbit."

Sure enough, in no time at all, here comes the rabbit just in front of the dogs. I raised the gun and fired, and I could see the pellets from the shell hit several feet behind the rabbit. I don't know if it was the sudden unexpected kick from this gun or the frustration of missing my first rabbit, but I said something that I hadn't said before, and it wasn't good. I had missed, and it only made the rabbit go that much faster. I would not get another shot. My dad only laughed at me and said there would be another time. He must have liked this adventure because he told this story to everyone around.

Times were still kind of bad, but I didn't know how bad because the good times hadn't been too good. I was now spending a lot of time with my dad and was beginning to grow up a little, even though I would always be the baby of the family.

Chapter 7: Dad's Illness

Dad had been somewhat healthy most of his life. He just had the occasional cold. He also was a very heavy smoker and drinker. I guess, from the smoking, he had developed a nagging cough. This had gotten a little worse over time. He smoked the roll yourself Prince Albert tobacco that came in a red can. And so did the rest of my family, except Louise and Momma. But we were all exposed to second hand smoke constantly. Louis, Buddy, and Bill smoked about as much as Dad, which was a lot. Dad smoked a pipe on special occasions that really would stink up the place. Louise, I think, kept this pipe for several years. He also smoked Bull Durham that came in a tie up bag, which was a little cheaper. He was now 63 years old.

A small knot came upon his lower neck area. After many weeks, this knot grew larger, and he finally went to the doctor in Pine Bluff. This doctor said he did not like what he saw and advised him to go to a specialist in Little Rock. Dad didn't take well to this and tried to avoid the issue, thinking all would be fine in time. However, this not only bothered him mentally, but also the lump was still growing.

Now was the time to seek further attention. He contacted the Pine Bluff doctor and told him there was no money and asked him what his options were. The doctor was kind enough to recommend the University of Arkansas Medical Center located in Little Rock, which, at that time, was a training center for new young doctors, and they would see patients on a pay-as-you-could basis.

So somehow dad got there. I am not sure how. I guess Buddy must have taken him.

They ran some tests and took a biopsy of the lump and sent Dad home. A few days later, the Medical Center sent dad the results. It was cancer, and he would need some more tests. What were we to do? I was not told about this until much later. However, kids can sense when things are not right. My whole family was torn up over this.

I think dad wanted to give up at this point, but the pain had begun. So back to the Medical Center he went. This time they would do surgery and remove the lump. But, when they operated, they found much more than they had expected. It was malignant, and the surgery would make it spread more rapidly. They said it was lung cancer, and they had done all that they could do for him. They gave him pain medicine and sent him home.

They tried to keep this information from me, but I could tell it was very bad. Mother and I stayed with Buddy and Laverne in Pine Bluff for a while, and Bill stayed at our house and continued to work. Buddy had a daughter, Shirley. She was only 2 years old. She and her granddad got along just fine. He thought she was just it. They would play and laugh together very much.

Laverne was very concerned with me. She would give me
25 cents to go to the movies. I had to walk there and back,
but that was fine, since I was used to this walking thing.
Back then, the movie was ten cents, and popcorn and a
Coke were a nickel each. What a deal! My wife and I just
went to a movie last week, and we spent about 30 dollars.
My, how times have changed!

After a couple of weeks, my dad began to feel a little
better. So Buddy carried us home. It seemed if my dad
wanted to spend some more time with me. He had
become very short winded. But as soon as he was up to it,
he took me on my last hunting trip with him. He called it a
coon hunt. I knew that this would be just a way for him to
take me on a short hunting trip because it was on a sunny
afternoon, and I had learned enough about coon hunting
to know that you did this at night with a carbide light and
coon dogs.

Anyway, we made the best of it. I knew that my dad did
not feel like hunting. So we just enjoyed as much of this
outing as we could. Indeed, this would be our last hunting
trip.

Dad got worse right after this trip. Buddy came and got us
to stay with him for a while. I remember that I was still
fairly small and for sure I was skinny. I slept in Shirley's
baby bed. It wasn't too bad if I stayed curled up. If I
straightened my legs, they would stick out between the
bedrails.

It wasn't many days until one morning I was awakened by some noise. My dad was asleep in a bed near the baby bed where I was sleeping. I remember, just as I opened my eyes, I saw my dad pass away. He just went still with his eyes open. Buddy immediately came over and said he was gone, and then Buddy took his hand and closed my daddy's eyes. They immediately got me out of the bed and into another room. This was January 7, 1955.

At first, there was talk about not letting me attend the funeral. Buddy told mom he thought I was old enough to understand, and I should go. Buddy went to the clothing store and bought me some new clothes for the funeral. These were the only new clothes that I can ever remember having. For some reason, Buddy bought me a hat. I certainly didn't need this hat. But, I guess it looked nice. Anyway I wore it to the funeral, but I don't think it got much wear after that.

I didn't know what to expect at the funeral. I saw my dad just lying there, as if he was asleep. He looked like he had been freed from his pain. I guess everything went as planned. I can remember, at the cemetery after they had covered the grave, we returned for our final goodbyes. I stood at the head of my father's grave and looked blank.

Psalms: 46:10

Be still and know I am God.

I remember that as I stood there, there was a piece of mind that came over me. It was in the middle of winter, and the weather and temperature were perfect. There was no wind stirring the trees. Everything was still. I had to remind myself that this was God's plan, even though at this early age, I hadn't learned much about God.

I didn't know what to think. I knew I was now without my father, and he wasn't coming back. Somehow we purchased a double gravesite here. My mother would be buried next to dad when she died several years later. I would just take life as it would come and make the best of it.

Chapter 8: Back to School

I was in fourth grade. When I returned to school, the teachers and students treated me with a lot of respect. It was evident that they had discussed this before I returned. I was the only one in my 4th grade class who did not have a father. I really didn't want any special attention. I think I would have made it much better if they had just pretended that everything was normal and nothing had happened. All of this attention just kept reminding me of this issue more and more.

I was only 10 years old and not really old enough to get any kind of job to help Bill support our family. They made it clear that we would be fine and that I was to stay in school and get my education. Bill was 19 years old and now head of my family. How would he handle this? Would he get frustrated and abandon us or find a girl and get married? All kinds of things were going through my mind.

I certainly had not become a Christian yet or know very much about God. I did not know what he was going to do for us. I just knew that the only way to get through this was to rely on my mother and hope that Bill would stay around. After all, he had been pretty well taking care of us, financially, anyway. Bill only made like $3.00 per day, working from daylight to dark on the farm, but he gave it to mom to buy food and a few clothes. We didn't need many clothes. We wore the ones that we had until they were completely worn out. I didn't need any shoes in the summertime, for I went barefooted.

They never bought me any new shoes. We bought used shoes from Dave Lupo's repair shop in Pine Bluff. Mr. Lupo took old shoes and put new soles on them for resale. I remember one time I picked out a pair of blue suede shoes. Mom bought them for me. I knew that I had to really like these shoes, for there would be no more until I wore these completely out. I think I wore these shoes for a couple years. I wore the suede right off of them. But I had something that none of my other school mates had. I don't think they ever made too much fun of them.

Bill began working for another farmer named William David (W.D.) Ferguson. Mr. Ferguson sold his cotton farmland and now only had a cattle farm. They were of the Black Angus breed. He also raised his own hay for winter food. The good thing about this is that Mr. Ferguson owned a house that was just behind Louis and Nadine's. We moved into this house, and now I was next door to my best buddies, Charles and Billy. We were the three musketeers. We lived there for several years.

Many times on Sunday afternoon, especially when Nadine had fried chicken for lunch, Nadine's sister and her husband would come from Pine Bluff to visit her. I don't know what her real name was because everyone called her "Ole Levy". She was a rather large lady. Her husband's name was Ed. Ole Levy and Ed attended church in Pine

Bluff. They made Sunday afternoon visits right after church, for they knew that Louis and Nadine would have fried chicken. The talk was, and I believe it may be true, that Ole Levy ate so much one day that her belly busted.

Louis and Nadine now had three more boys, Jimmy (Tinker) Lewis, Roger Dale, and Danny Lee. We almost could have our own baseball team.

Buddy went on to have the largest family. He had a total of seven children. He had five boys and two girls. Other than Shirley, he had Mike, Larry David, Jimmy, Karen, Bobby, and Terry (Butch).

Laverne; Charles (Buddy)

Larry; Mike; Shirley

The house that we had moved into wasn't much at all. It was a typical farm hand house. Except this was what they called a "shotgun" house. It was narrow with three rooms in a row. It didn't stand straight up. It had a slight lean to it. There was no pump for water. We had to carry our water from Louis' house, which was only a little ways down the road. This was a daily chore. Louis had what we called a pitcher pump. Every time you wanted to get water from the pump, you had to find a little water to pour into it for priming. You poured this water into the top of the pitcher and then pumped real fast. After a while, the suction would catch, and the water would come out of the pitcher spout. You had to keep pumping until you obtained all the water you wanted because if you ever stopped pumping, the pump would lose prime, and you would have to start all over again.

We had what we called a rain barrel that was placed beside our house. It had a tin down spout extending from the roof. When it rained, the run off from the roof filled the barrel, and we would not have to tote as much water. We used this for washing our clothes.

In the winter months, we had an old potbelly wood-burning stove to keep us warm. It had a large pipe that went up through the ceiling and on out through the roof. This allowed most of the smoke to exit the stove and the house. Even with this, our clothes still had that smoky smell. It worked really well, as long as you kept it full of wood. It was my job to keep the wood by the stove. I would go across the river levee and get some of the smaller willow trees that had fallen down and dried out. I pulled them all the way home and cut them into firewood with our old dull axe. Each night, I gathered a stack of wood and placed it behind our old potbellied stove. Remember, I said willow wood. This was not the best kind of wood to burn. It would burn like paper, which is very fast. We used this because that was all we had. I had no way to cut down any of the hardwood trees, such as oak or hickory. These trees would have been like gold to me, for they would hold a fire for a very long time.

We had what they called a slinging blade. This was a flat blade with cutting teeth on each side and a handle. I was now old enough to use this to cut the grass in our yard. At least I could keep it from getting too tall. It was lot of hard work and sweat, but I got her done.

We still had our iron bedsteads and coal oil cook stove. We only used two of the three rooms. The back room was not much. Some of the boards were torn off the sides, and this exposed the room to the weather elements. We now had an icebox. This was like a refrigerator without any electricity. An ice truck came by weekly, and if we had any money, mom would buy a 50 pound block of ice. It would keep for a couple of days, if we didn't open the icebox door very often.

Bill was pretty creative. He made us a chair and a small couch from some old boards. Mother then made some cushions from some of her quilting materials. She covered these, so they kind of matched our quilts. The inside wall in our house looked pretty bad. There was no paint. Bill took some cornstarch and mixed in some water to make a paste. Then he pasted some old newspapers on the wall. It didn't look very good, but it was unique. If you ever got bored, you could just read some of the newspaper articles right off the wall.

At night, especially during the summer months, we had to deal with the mosquitoes. They were really bad because there were rice fields filled with water surrounding our house. Momma used a hand pump sprayer of DDT to spray the entire house. This helped out a little, but the DDT smell almost got to us. Somehow, some of the mosquitoes found a way to survive. Trying to go to sleep was quite a chore. These mosquitoes would sing you to sleep on most nights. Sometimes, even during hot weather, we had to cover our heads with the quilts just to get to sleep. This would keep the mosquitoes from biting us. I guess the sweating was better than the mosquito bites.

I can remember another very fascinating thing. There was a military base located just north of Pine Bluff. It was called the Pine Bluff Arsenal. This site was used for bomb testing. Each afternoon around 4:00, they would begin their testing. This testing site was not very far from our house, as the crow flies. It was over the levee just beyond the Arkansas River. The noise would shake the windows in our house. You could see the cloud of smoke as it mushroomed high into the sky. This arsenal is still there today. They have been destroying the chemical weapons on site.

Bill walked about a mile to work. Then he walked back and forth for lunch and back home at night. This gave him at least four miles per day of walking. Sometimes, Mr. Ferguson would drive him home for lunch and wait in the car for him to finish eating. I think he did this mostly just to enjoy some of mother's fresh yeast rolls. On the special days that she made these, she would take a couple of these hot, buttered rolls to Mr. Ferguson's car for him to enjoy while Bill finished his lunch. Mother said the weather had to be just right for her to cook these rolls. There was something about the sun or air, or maybe the humidity that had to be just right for the yeast in the bread to rise correctly. Anyway, she had this system figured out pretty well. My mom was a great cook.

Bill worked hard, but he just made enough money for us to get by, nothing more. In the summertime, I worked some for Mr. Ferguson. I liked to work. Up until now, I had not been qualified to do much work. Remember, I was still the baby of the family. I would see Bill come home all greasy and grimy. So I thought the more grease that I got on me, the more that would signify that I was a hard worker.

Occasionally I was allowed to help in the hay field. I remember on one occasion I was helping Bill. We had to hook two trailers together to take them to the barn. He told me to stand in front of the second trailer and hold the trailer tongue up so that he could attach the tongue of this trailer to the rear of the other trailer. I did this, and as he was backing up, he could not see me. I could not see the connection holder under the front trailer, and as the two of them were coming together, I missed the connection, and they came together right on my forearms. I was pinned between the two trailers. I screamed out loud enough for Bill to hear me, and he immediately stopped and pulled the trailers apart. I can still see the look on Bill's face when he came around to see what had happened. He was in a panic. This could have certainly been a **"Turn in Life" or even a life-ending experience**. I was fine. My thighs had cushioned the blow just enough so that I hadn't broken any bones. I was just badly bruised on the top of both of my forearms. The raw wood on the end of the trailer bed had made an indention into my arms. I can still see this indented area on my arms today. Bill, with no medical training, got some gasoline and poured it on my arms. Please do not try this at home! I guess he was thinking that this was just as good as alcohol or something. It stung like crazy. But, other than being sore for a few days, I was fine.

Many times, I worked for Mrs. Thelma; this was W.D.'s wife. She hired me to pull the weeds from her flowerbeds. I hated this work, but I was paid two dollars a day. Most of the time, I never worked an entire day at this. Therefore, I only earned a few cents.

Looking back, this could have been a real good part time profession for me to invest in for my future. Today, there are lawn and garden services everywhere in my neighborhood. I learned from the ground up and became very good at this yard type work. As I grew a little older, I mowed the Ferguson yard, which was very large. It had an extended front yard, with flowerbeds and trees everywhere that I had to mow around. This was sort of difficult for me because I was still kind of skinny. The mower was a two-wheel push type with rotary blades. Sometimes, I could barely push it. It took me most of the day to mow this yard. After mowing, I would have to go back over the yard and pull the old cattail weeds that the push mower would not cut. These were too tall, and the mower blades would just push them down, and then they would pop right back up. I carried along a paper sack for these weeds. I got a dollar for the mowing, and I mowed about every other week.

Out in the area near the cow pasture, there was a wooded area that was called the graveyard. In this area, there were many old Indian graves with markers with dates of over 100 years old. The area was kind of spooky. It had many trees. Some were cedar, and others were hard wood. The graveyard even had a few pecan trees in it that produced those very tiny pecans. They were small, but they sure were delicious. With all of these trees being there in the graveyard, many leaves fell and covered the ground. Mrs. Ferguson asked me to go there and rake back some of those leaves and dig up some of that good, rich top soil for her flowerbeds. I did this, but I didn't like it. I certainly made sure that I didn't dig very deep and accidentally dig up some of those old Indian bones.

Also in this graveyard area were some plants that were called "Indian turnips". I guess this was because they looked like turnips. Anyway, Bill and Louis like to use these Indian turnips to entice people for fun. These turnips were a little different. They would cut off a little section of the turnip and dare you to eat it. Of course, back then, the dare was taken seriously. When you placed the turnip in your mouth, it would taste fine. As a matter of fact, it had very little turnip taste to it. In just a short period of time, it would begin to burn your mouth. The longer you chewed it, the hotter it got. You would have to spit it out, but that would not stop the burning. Your mouth would get hotter and hotter. You would have to take something and rub your tongue with it and wash your mouth out just to survive. Then, the heat would linger for a couple of days. Bill and Louis seemed to really enjoy seeing someone suffer this Indian turnip episode whenever they could con someone into taking a bite. See how much fun we had way back then? You would be surprised at how many people would try to eat a bite of this turnip just to prove how tough they were.

Sometimes when I helped out with the cows, just for fun, I would catch a small calf and get on his back and play like I was a professional bull rider. I learned the hard way to make sure I picked out a very small calf. These calves were very strong, and they didn't like having a rider on their backs. I got thrown off many times, but it was fun.

Most of the time, I would go to work with Bill just to have
something to do. I helped him where I could, but there
would be no pay. The cows had to be rounded up for their
medicine or shots. We herded them into a fenced in chute.
We had no horses; we just did this on foot. I was small, but
I think most of the cows respected me. I helped to herd
these cows into the chute. Sometimes, after they entered
it, they would stall, and they didn't want to move on to the
front for their shot and medicine. We had what they called
a "shocker stick" to move them along. When it was placed
on their rears, it changed their minds real quickly, and they
could not wait to move forward.

Bill helped Mr. Ferguson bale hay each summer. This hay
was stored for food for the cows to eat during the winter
months. One time, after baling a field of hay, it rained
really hard, and all the bales got wet. We could not store
this hay until it dried out because it would mold quickly.
When the sun came out, the top side of the bales dried.
Now the bales had to be turned over for the underside of
the hay bales to dry out. Mr. Ferguson hired me for this
job. Oh boy, more money! Wait a minute; it wasn't that
easy. First, I had to walk from the tractor shop to the hay
field. This was no easy chore, for I was scared of the horses
in the pasture that I had to cross to get to the hay field. I
don't think they were going to hurt me. But I will never
know. Each time I entered this horse pasture, the horses
charged toward me. My guess is that they were thinking
that I was bringing them food. Anyway, I didn't like this. I

ran as fast as I could to get away from them. Have you ever tried to outrun a horse? It is not easy.

The next dilemma I faced on this project was turning the hay bales over. I think every bale of hay had at least one snake or lizard under it. I pushed the hay bales over and jumped back and ran away a little. This had to be a sight for someone to see. There were about 50 bales of hay for me to turn. I did them all the same way. I continued to push and jump back and run a little. I guess I did all right, since I never got snake bit or lizard bit.

Soon after my dad died, Bill received his draft notice for the Army. Back then, every male had to register for the draft at the age of 18. If you were single, you would be drafted for a two-year stint in the Army. If you volunteered, you would serve four years. If you were married, you didn't have to serve.

After Bill got his notice, Mr. Ferguson said that he would talk with the draft board and tell them Bill's situation. He would tell them that Bill was single, but he was serving as the head of the household. This was acceptable, and Bill didn't get drafted. This would have been a **"Turn in Life"** experience for me. What would we have done if Bill had gone into the Army?

Bill Frye

My family had learned to make a living the hard way, and looking back, they had some crude ideas about most things. For instance, on my birthday, I was allowed to stay home from school and pick cotton and keep the money as my birthday present. There were no mechanical cotton pickers during this time. You straddled the row with a long cotton sack between your legs and picked cotton out of the cotton bowls and placed it into the sack. Most pickers could pick only about one hundred pounds of cotton a day. I never picked very much, but now I would have a few cents in my pocket. I think we got about 3 cents per pound for picking the cotton. This meant a lot to me, but there wasn't much for me to spend this money on.

There was a rolling store that came by our place. It was a truck that had an enclosed bed on it, kind of like a tall camper shell today. In this rolling store were all kinds of dry goods and some candy. This is where my extra money came in handy. Boy, this candy sure was good.

Since we lived right by Louis, I had kids to play with because he had several of all ages. Charles, Billy, and I grew up together. We played every day that I was at home and was not fishing with my dad. There were a couple of hay barns that we played in. We played hide and seek in there. We also had several friendly wrestling matches. We would have hay all over us and in our clothes and hair. Yes, I had hair way back then!

Sherrill School was a lot of fun, and I had many friends. Just before school would be out for the summer each year, there was a picnic day. It seemed that every year we went to Oakland Park in Pine Bluff. Each student signed up to bring a picnic item. I signed up to bring a jar of pickles or a bag of potato chips.

This was a fun day, but as fate would have it, I would have to be sick on some of these days and not get to attend the picnic. One year on this date, I had the chicken pox. The very next year, I had the measles. How could this happen? I just stayed home and cried and ate my bag of potato chips.

Charles; Johnny; Billy;

Mike; Larry

Another one of the Ferguson's relatives lived near Louis and Nadine. Her name was Susie (Poe) Ferguson. She was a very kind lady and just about took Rosemary (Cissi) in to raise her. Cissi spent a lot of time over at her house. Poe lived in a very nice large farmhouse surrounded by mulberry trees. It was just a beautiful place. Poe lived alone and had no car. W.D. took her wherever she wanted to go. I remember he picked her up every Sunday morning, and they went to Pine Bluff for church. Poe's house was on wooden blocks. Us boys crawled up under her house and listened to Poe talk to herself. This was a lot of fun.

Poe's house also had electricity and a telephone. She had a party line. There were several people in the neighborhood who had phones. They were all on the same phone line. Each one had a certain number of short and long rings.

This was very comical because when the phone rang, you would know whom the ring belonged to, and you could pick up the phone and listen in on the conversation. This was not very nice. When we got a call, you could hear others picking up their phones to listen in. They didn't have to say a word. You could just hear them breathing. I guess this was their social media back then.

Poe also had a large front yard near the main road, which, when we were growing up, was gravel. The county graded it regularly and kept this road in fairly good shape. We played baseball here and hit the ball toward the road. I think this may have been a little dangerous, but way back then, there was not much traffic. As we grew older and could hit the ball farther, it would go over the road onto the side of the levee that was just beyond the road ditch. I can remember beating down all of the grass on the side of the levee, searching for our baseball. We didn't have many baseballs. They were hard to come by. We played with one ball until all of the leather came off of it and then played with it some more, until it was no longer considered a ball.

We played a game called flys and skinners. There was one batter, and everyone else played out in the field, and after catching three fly balls or seven skinners (ground balls), you become the next batter. We would do this until everyone was tired out.

There was an old man named Fred Lassiter who traveled this road frequently. He stayed drunk most of the time. He would stop his truck right in the middle of this road and take a nap. Everyone knew Fred, and they would just go right around him. After a while, Fred would wake up and go on down the road until he needed another nap. Fred got so bad at this that his sisters took his truck away from him. They feared that he might hurt himself or others. They all lived together. After they took his truck away, Fred would get on his small Alice Chambers tractor and do the same thing again. I think Fred did this until the day he died.

On many Sunday afternoons, Buddy, Laverne, and the kids came to visit us. He had purchased an old Studebaker car. It was a funny looking thing. It was pointed on each end and kind of looked like a space ship or something. They would bring us a new ball to play with. It was a special time for us. We had more kids to play on our team. One Sunday, Buddy really surprised me and brought me a pair of cowboy boots. I thought these were the greatest thing that I had ever gotten. They were way too small for me, but I could get them on, and that was enough. I wore these boots everywhere. My feet were sore and my toes would hurt, but I wore those boots and suffered the consequences.

Another thing that we did may seem a little strange to most. Buddy would sometimes bring me some firecrackers when he came to visit. He and I played chicken with these. We would light one of these firecrackers in our hands and toss it at each other's feet. Please do not try this at home!

We knew this was dangerous; however, I don't remember any major issues. We had a few of the firecrackers to go off in our hands while lighting them. This made for an unpleasant feeling for a couple of days. Of course, this would end our chicken playing until later. The old thumbnail would turn black, and sometimes it would peel off. (And this was fun?)

On Easter one year, Buddy bought Momma some colored baby chickens. She enjoyed having these chickens. Everyone said that one of the yellow ones was a rooster. She took special care of this baby rooster. She named this rooster "Pete". Pete lived a couple of years with Momma's special tender loving care. Old Pete followed Momma around the yard and would sit down next to her. The odd thing about old Pete was that as she grew older, we could tell that old Pete was not going to be an old rooster because old Pete was a hen after all. It made no difference to Momma; she still called the old hen, "old Pete". Old Pete finally died of old age, but this chicken lived the life of riley. She was taken care of very well.

Mother always seemed to be very fond of all the farm animals. Mr. Ferguson would let her take care of one of his calves from time to time. Bill built a pen right up against our house for Momma to keep this calf near her. The side of our house served as one side of the pen. The calf could see right into our house. On several occasions, it would actually lick the windowpane. This created quite a mess, as you can imagine. Mother would nurture and pet this calf more than you can believe. She had an old rubber glove that she placed over the top of a bottle to feed the calf some milk. She would cut a fingertip of the rubber glove and let the calf suck the milk. She always hated to give the calf up when it became time for them to go to the pasture. I never knew why she did this because it always made her sad to give the animals up.

There were always many stray dogs in our neighborhood. When the city people got rid of their dogs, they brought them out to the country and just turned them loose to fend for themselves. If you ever gave these stray dogs any food, they would not go away. Therefore, there were many dogs around us kids. I kind of took one in to be my special pet. This dog was a cross breed between a cocker spaniel and who knows what else. I kept this dog for several years. We became buddies, and I took special care of it. I named her "Lassie" after the TV dog. Of course, she was not a collie like the TV Lassie, but I liked the name. Lassie followed me everywhere. There was no Dog Chow. We couldn't afford any store bought dog food. Lassie and the other stray dogs just had to find their own food or table scraps that we tossed out to them. Most of the time, the dogs knew when the table scraps would be tossed out, and they would be ready for the fight that was about to occur. Many times, I just put Lassie's food in a separate place so that she would not have to endure the fight, even though she could hold her own with most of the big dogs. I kept Lassie for several years. She just ran free, for there was never any fence to keep her from danger. When she got older, she liked to chase cars. Then, one day, she got run over on the gravel road. Lassie lived a good life and gave me very much enjoyment.

By now Buddy had to find another job because the beer company where he had been working went out of business. It didn't take him very long to find more work. Sunbeam Bread Company hired him, and he worked there many years until retirement.

One summer, I went to stay with Buddy and Laverne for a few days. Buddy knew how much I liked to fish. He said that he would take me down to the Arkansas River on his way to work, and I could fish there all day. Then he would pick me up after he got off. This was great for me. Buddy took me to the Pine Bluff City dump area to fish. Now, this would be quite an experience. Buddy said that he had heard of people catching some really large catfish in this area. I guess it was a great feeding area for the giant catfish.

There were no landfills back then. The city hauled their garbage to the river and dumped it on the bank. Then they took a bulldozer and pushed it into the river. The river current washed the garbage on down steam, and it would deteriorate or go away somewhere.

In those days, people seemed to believe that their garbage somehow melted into the landscape and disappeared. Or it simply went away. It sounds odd from today's perspective. It's as if "away" were some mythical, Oz-like place where all waste, trash, and associated ugliness could be disposed of without consequence. And we threw stuff away until it was piled higher than the fence around it, or it killed the fish, or it put a haze on the horizon.

It has taken us a shameful long while, but at last we have learned that there is no place such as "away." It's simply delusional to think there is or ever was such a place as "away".

The fact is the planet Earth is a closed system. Whenever and wherever a light switch is thrown, a puff of smoke or some type of pollution is created when power is generated. We may not see it, but it's there. My trash washes up on somebody else's shore or fouls their ground water, just as surely as air pollution follows prevailing winds into the valley. Just think how far we have come today, yet how far we have to go in this area of waste and pollution.

One time, I can remember that we were flying a kite in Bulb's front yard. The wind was not blowing near enough for it, but we were determined. We got it in the air somehow, and the kite landed on top of Louis' house. Bulb had an idea that he could get it down. He tied a brick to the end that he was holding and threw the brick over the house into the back yard. It worked, but mother had just stepped out of the back door, and it struck her right on the head. She went down, and blood was everywhere. Louis got in the truck and took her to the hospital, located in Pine Bluff. She would be just fine-she just needed several stiches. I thought for sure that Bulb had killed my mother. I think he may have gotten the beating of his life, but he got all right evidentially.

Another fun thing that we kids did was play on the levee across the gravel road. We had some sheets of tin and some cardboard boxes that we used to slide down the levee into the ditch. This WAS fun. Sometimes we would tumble over, but that was fine; the ditch would stop us when we reached the bottom of the levee.

Louis and Bill would play cards with us kids. We were taught to play spades or smut. They would hold a tin plate over a flame on the cook stove until the bottom of it turned black or was all covered with smut. Each player would then be allowed to take his finger and rub some of the black smut on it, and then each player would make a smut mark on the loser's face. This produced some very interesting looking faces by the end of the game. I thought this was fun.

Louis left the farm landlord where he had worked for several years, and he went to work on the Arkansas River as a tugboat deck hand. He eventually learned the trade of tugboat operator. His first job was to help build and distribute wooden mats that were placed along the riverbank to keep it from eroding during the spring flooding season.

A couple of times Bulb, Billy, and I would get to go with
Louis and hang out on the barge that his tug boat would
be pushing down the river. This was cool. We had to be
very careful, for these barges didn't have any safety rails.
We helped Louis out a little after we learned to tie the
special seaman's knot to secure the barges, so they would
not be washed downstream by the river current. I think at
that time we all three had decided that we wanted to be
tugboat operators when we grew up. This was fun but
hard work. The river had no locks or dams, and the current
was very swift most of the time, especially in the early
spring. The swirling water would create suck holes as it
flowed. During this time, the river rose really high and
became very dangerous. The riverbanks eroded badly. You
could hear the steep dirt riverbanks caving in all up and
down the river. It made a very loud crashing sound. Here is
where the wooden river mats were placed to help reduce
the erosion. They wouldn't stop it, but they would greatly
reduce it.

Louis was paid a much larger salary than he got on the
farm. It wasn't long before he purchased a used Ford car. I
thought this was just a neat car. Louis would take Mom
and me to town with his family on Saturday to buy some
groceries. This was great, except every time we were on
the way home he would say, "I am going to stop at the
beer joint for a beer." I learned very quickly that this
meant that he would drink many beers, and we would be

there until closing time. Louis loved to drink beer and play shuffleboard.

I don't think he ever got really drunk, but he would swerve a little on the drive home. My real concern was that we had to cross the Arkansas River Bridge, which was a single lane with a stoplight to alert the oncoming traffic. It was pretty narrow, but we seemed to always just make it home.

One Saturday night or early Sunday morning on the way home from the beer joint, it happened. Louis, Nadine, and Mom were in the front seat. The rest of us kids were in the back seat. Some of us were standing up between the seats as we all liked to do so that we could get a better view of the road. There were no seat belts back then. The car was full of people. We sideswiped another car not too far from home. It was on my side. Now this could have been a **"Turn in Life"** or a life-ending experience for all of us. Nobody stopped, and everyone was all right. The next morning, we learned that the other car belonged to a friend who lived just up the road from us. He had been drinking also. So life goes on.

Not long after this incident, Louis traded the Ford for an old Chevrolet pickup truck. This was good to be used around the farm, but when we went to town on Saturday night, all of the kids had to ride in the back. It's hard to believe that as many times as we did this, I can never remember it raining on us. We just had to sit out in front of the beer joint in the back of this truck while Louis had his beers until closing time. Boy, I hated this.

For some reason, just before we left town, we would make a stop at a store called the College Grocery to get our meat, which was a pound of bologna. Sometimes, when they had some extra money, they went next door to a place they called the Chinaman's and bought a couple of pork chops. Both of these items were gone pretty fast. By Monday, we were back to beans and potatoes and mostly beans.

Sometimes we got to stay home on Saturday afternoon, while Louis, Nadine, and Mom went to town. Charles, Billy, and me always found something to keep us busy, especially in the summertime. We would go swimming in one of the bar pits across the levee. These were only mud holes about three feet deep, and mud about another foot deep. There were some snakes, but they didn't bother us, and we didn't bother them. None of us could swim, and we could not learn to swim in this shallow water. There were no swimming trunks. We swam naked because if we didn't, we would get our underwear wet. Then our parents would know that we had been swimming. That would not have been a good thing, for we would have gotten the beating of our lives. The water was so muddy that when we came out of it, the scum covered what little hair we had on our bodies. That was fine though, for we learned if we let it dry a little, we could just brush it off.

We soon decided that we had to find some deeper water in order to learn to swim. So, the next time we had a chance, the rice canal right behind our house was the place. Here is where we all learned to swim. This canal was just right, and if the water pump was running, the water would be clear. It was just very cold. But that wouldn't bother us for long. We jumped in on one side, and we figured if we could make it to the other side, we would be swimming. The depth of the water in the middle of the canal would be just over our heads. We all agreed if we could make it across the canal, we had to swim a little bit. We all made it!

Each of us boys had an old tire that had been taken off the rim. We rolled these tires everywhere. We made believe that these were our cars. When we went into the house, we parked our tires right outside by the front porch until we were ready to leave. Then here we would go again.

One day, we gathered some old 2x4 boards and built us each a set of tom walkers or stilts. We took one of the long boards and nailed a short piece of wood onto the side of it for a foothold. Of course, we had to make two of these, one for each foot. The footholds were about 24" off the ground. It took us several tries to use these, but we finally mastered it, somewhat. We walked all over the place with these things. It is a wonder that we didn't break a leg or something. We did get our share of bruises. We got good enough at walking with the tom walkers that we could climb up some steps. Going down was a real problem that we never over came.

We had another pastime event. We nailed a lard can lid through the center and attached it to a long stick so that it could spin. Then we rolled this apparatus along as we walked from place to place. This was fun. The Frye boys were very creative. We made our own fun.

In a few weeks, we had some company come to visit us for a few days. This was my mother's sister, Ruth from Maryland. She and her husband, George Pennington, the peg legged postman, came to visit. This was great, but we only had a two-room house. We survived, and I cannot tell you how we all stayed in this house.

They wanted us to show them around everywhere. That was a great deal too, but we hadn't been anywhere. They wanted to go to Hot Springs and get some of the hot water. We did that and had a great time. They were fascinated with the cotton fields. On the way home from Hot Springs, I remember Uncle George stopped near a field that had some pickers near the road. Uncle George, pegged leg and all, got his camera and took some pictures of the people picking cotton. He told them that they might be on the evening news. That got them very excited. Of course this didn't happen. It was just Uncle Georges' way of having some fun. He told everyone about this.

Chapter 9: Welfare Help

Mother began having some black out spells. She would just be sitting in a chair, and she would begin to stare or try to pull something from the air. During this time, she would not respond to anyone who talked to her. She would just be blank. After working with her for a few minutes, she would come around, but she would feel really bad for a couple of days. I thought maybe this problem had something to do with Charles' brick throwing escapade. After all, he had hit her right in the head with the brick.

We asked Mr. Ferguson to take her to the doctor to have her checked out. The diagnoses came back that she had epilepsy, and this illness would be with her for the rest of her life. She should never be left alone. They gave her some medicine to somewhat control the disease, but indeed, this was with her for the rest of her life. How were we to afford this medicine?

Mary (Mother) E. Frye

Mr. Ferguson took us to the welfare office to fill out an application for help. We qualified. They would help with the medication, give mother twenty dollars a month, and we also qualified for the commodity program. This was embarrassing to our family, and we didn't want the handout. We wanted to support ourselves without any help. After a couple of months on our own, we found that the price of mother's medication was more than we could afford. So, we accepted the welfare offer.

I think they paid for most of the medication, and the twenty dollars came in real handy. I had to get my school principal to write a letter to the welfare office, stating that I was attending school. I really hated to do this. I had to do this every year that I remained in school. I never got used to this, but each year, I would get it done. Bill also had to have his employer write a letter, stating that he was supporting his mother and me. He also had to get an income statement for the welfare committee to review. We went to the fairgrounds in Pine Bluff and received our commodity hand out. We got what they had for the month. Most of the time, they had cheese, rice, powdered milk, and flour or cornmeal. I never got so tired of powdered milk in my life, but we were really grateful for this help. The twenty-dollar check came in handy in more ways than anyone could ever imagine.

In the summer months, I did some yard work for Mrs. Thelma, chopped some cotton, helped with the hay harvest, or helped Bill with the cows. I liked the hay harvest the best. It was very hot on most days that we hauled the hay from the fields to the barn for storage. We got all dirty and sweaty. But I kind of liked the hard work. It made me feel like I was contributing to the family. We were making the best of it. We still didn't have much, but, we were still family and enjoyed each other as much as we could.

One fall season, the blackbirds invaded the rice fields. Bill decided we would try a blackbird pie. He went out in the field and with only one shot from his shotgun, he got several blackbirds. They were very plentiful. He had to have a whole bunch of birds because they were very small. Mother cooked the pie. I didn't care much for it. I think Bill ate most of it. On a few occasions, Mother would make a vinegar pie. She would put a lot of sugar in it, but I remember it was still very tart. I could eat this. But, I made a decision that I would stay with the beans and potatoes and mostly beans. These beans would sometimes create a lot of gas around our house. One time, it got so bad that Mom had to put baking soda in them to sort of calm down the gas. Bill and I had a good time with this. We thought it was funny.

Soon, the people from Sherrill Baptist Church visited us and invited us to attend their church. We had never been to church before. I thought it was great that these people wanted us to come to their church. They said they were starting a bus route and could pick us up on Sunday morning and take us to Sunday school and church and then bring us home. All of us kids wanted to go. So, the adults told us we could go, and we did. None of the grownups ever went.

We attended most every Sunday for several months. No one ever told us how to be saved or what we needed to do to become Christians. We didn't know very much of what they were talking about, since we had never been to church before. One thing that I can remember is that some of the mothers in our Sunday school class took us to Pine Bluff to appear on a TV show. The show was called "The Herb Herring Show". We were all very excited about this. We were now celebrities. We also participated in the Christmas play and in Bible School, but never really got the hang of this church thing. I think they were teaching us about the Bible, but we weren't paying much attention. After a while, we began to drop out, and soon we didn't go at all. We attended as long as we did because the family thought it was a great idea. We all knew there was a God; we just didn't know anything about being a Christian. Mother was encouraging. She knew the verses of some of the Christian hymns. She hummed them often. So she must have been exposed to church somewhere along the line. She never attended church, but she encouraged me to attend. This encouragement will come into play later in my life, that's for sure.

There seemed to always be a few presents at Christmas time. Mother always seemed to find a way to get me something for Christmas. We never talked much about what Christmas was all about, other than this was Jesus' birthday. She kept my present under her bed next to the wall. I could see it, but I never attempted to open it and ruin her pleasure of my surprise on Christmas. We always got to open our presents on Christmas Eve night. Bill took me rabbit hunting while mother got the presents ready. After a little while, Bill and I returned from hunting, and there it was. Santa Claus had been there, and I had missed seeing him again.

One year, I got a rubber Farmall tractor for Christmas. I played and played with this tractor. The wheels on the front were very close together and kind of weak. After a while, they broke off. I had to have this tractor in good condition because I played with this thing for hours upon hours. I made plenty of make believe farm fields with this rubber tractor. To replace the wheels, I took one of mother's empty thread spools and wired it on to the front of the tractor. It worked like new; it just didn't look very good.

I guess the best present I ever got was a BB gun. Just before Christmas one year, Bill asked me what I wanted. I knew that I couldn't have it, but I said a BB gun. Guess what? I got it! I felt really bad about this at first because I knew that Bill could not afford to buy the BB gun for me. I knew that he had to do without something he needed for me to get this BB gun. What a big brother he was! Not just that, he was a father to me now.

I thought that I could really fine-tune my shooting skills with this BB gun. I soon found out that no two bb bullets ever came out of the barrel the same way. Therefore, to just come close to the target was a chore. I shot at many birds, and I don't think that I ever hit one.

At around 12 years old, I begin to learn how to drive. Of course, we had no vehicle. Bill would occasionally let me ride on the farm tractor with him. I loved to do this. Sometimes he would let me drive a little. Yes, I was learning to drive. Louis would let Charles and Billy drive his truck a little, and when I was around he would let me have a turn. There was no automatic shifter, just a stick shift with a clutch. You had to time the clutch and gas petal just right. If not, the truck jerked ahead real fast, and sometimes it would go dead. It didn't take long to master this driving thing. I would drive a little for the next few years. Then, when I turned 16, I would get a driver license.

Things began to look up once again. Louis got electricity in his house, and it wasn't long before he bought a Magnavox black and white television set. There was no color, yet. It had rabbit ears for the antenna, and you could get one channel pretty well. There were two other channels that we could see if we wanted to endure the snowy screen. Bill, Mom, and I visited Louis about every night to watch TV. Our favorite shows were: *Gunsmoke, Amos and Andy, Roy Rogers and Dale Evans, The Three Stooges, The Little Rascals, Laurel and Hardy*, and *Howdy Doody*. We kids could not wait to get home from school to watch TV. We had to do our homework first, and then, we could watch TV until bedtime. All of the TV programs would go off the air at midnight. Of course, we did not stay up that late very many times. What a life we now had!

A few months later, Louis got an outside antenna for the TV. This helped a lot with the reception. We could now get all three channels. Sometimes, you would have to go outside and turn the antenna a little bit. But there was always a good reception; we just had to find the correct position. This antenna got turned almost daily. It seemed that the reception changed from day to day. But, it was still much better than the old rabbit ears on top of the TV set.

After a few months, we even got electricity at our house. Now we could have electric lights and get rid of the coal oil lamps. They had to install a light pole in our yard for us to have the electricity. I think this light pole and wire helped hold up our leaning house. For several years, everyone said that the only thing that kept this house from falling down was the light wire. You remember that when we first moved in, it was leaning rather badly, and it hadn't gotten any better over time. However, it never fell down while we lived there.

Chapter 10: The Allison Farm

Not long after this, Bill was offered a job on the Allison Rice Farm that was located over on the McKinney Road. This was around 1957.

Gas was 31¢/gal.

Bread was 19¢

A New car was $2100

Milk was $1.00/gal.

Postage stamps were3¢

The Stock market was at 436

I was going on 13 years old and in the seventh grade at the Sherrill Barrett School. This school had grades up through junior high school or through the 9th grade, and then they transferred the students to Altheimer High School several miles away.

Bill took this job and here we go moving again. This wasn't good. I was moving away from my nephews, my favorite playmates. The good thing was that we all would be still going to the same school. I was somewhat excited about this change. We would have a much better house that wasn't about to fall down. The house that we moved into was a much larger house. It had two bedrooms, although we had never needed more than one bedroom. We were fine with this. We didn't have enough furniture to fill this house, so we just shut off some of the rooms. It did have electricity and an electric well pump. This gave us running water into the kitchen sink. It was all cold water, since there was no hot water heater, yet. Somebody thought that we now needed a water softener for the hard water. What was the deal? We had been drinking and bathing in this hard water all of our lives. We also had a place for a butane stove. Now we could replace that old coal oil cook stove with a gas cooker. There was no bathroom, so the outhouse was still in play here. After we lived here for a few months, Bill decided that we could afford a small black and white television set. It had rabbit ears, and we could get one station fairly well. Now we were living again.

This house had been moved from the Pine Bluff Arsenal, and it was constructed well. The front yard was kind of large. We still had no lawn mower, so it was back to the old slinging blade.

I liked this place, and Mr. and Mrs. G.W. Allison were very kind people. They were a young couple. They kind of took me in for a few years. They had no children of their own. I think they believed that they were not going to have any kids. Mrs. Allison was now the second grade school teacher at Sherrill. She would keep a check on me at school.

Mr. Allison hired me to mow their yard. He paid me $1.50, and they had a power lawn mower that I could use. Yes! Yes! Sometimes there was no gas available for the mower.

I had to siphon some from a tractor or farm truck. I took a small section of a garden hose and placed one end into the gas tank and the other end into my mouth. I then sucked on it until the hose filled with gas. When the gas began to flow, I had to hold the end of it low in order for gravity to keep it going. I learned this siphon process pretty quickly. I remember a couple of times, I kept the hose in my mouth a little too long, and I would get a mouth full of gasoline. Now, this was not a good thing. But, it was what it was. I just had to spit the gas out as quickly as possible and rinse my mouth out with some water. What a fire hazard this must have been! A couple of times, I got a little dizzy from the gas fumes, but everything settled down after a couple of minutes. Please do not try this at home!

Whenever I got the opportunity, I helped out in the rice fields. Sometimes I got paid for pulling up the coffee beans that were scattered through the field. The coffee bean seeds would contaminate the rice harvest. Many times, there were too many of them to pull. I would then take a heavy portable sprayer and strap it onto my back. I used this to spray the beans with poison. This sprayer contained 2-4D. This is now banned from use. I think I inhaled my share of it. The overspray would get on my lips. It had a bitter taste. Now you get the picture. How could I end up normal? It seems that the deck was always stacked against me.

Mr. Allison had some friends that lived near Plum Bayou. One year, these friends spent most of the summer in

Europe. Mr. Allison asked me to go over and mow their yard every two weeks. This was great. It meant more money for me. After about two weeks, I begin to smell something really bad. It turned out that they had a large freezer full of food in one of the out buildings, and somehow the electricity had gone off. All of the food had spoiled. What a mess this was. We opened the freezer and removed all of this smelly spoiled food. I almost could not stand this. We didn't know what to do with the food. Bill and Mr. Allison decided to bury it in the edge of the cotton field near the house. This was fine, except I don't think we buried this mess deep enough. The very next night, some animals dug it up, and we had another major mess on our hands. It was scattered all over the place. We liked to have never got all this stuff cleaned up. The entire area around this house was a stinky mess for some time. After this, I dreaded going there to mow the yard. It took all summer for this stink to go away. I am glad that they didn't have any real close neighbors. If so, they would have had to abandon their homes for a while.

I helped Bill sometimes with the levee project in the rice fields. In order to flood the fields with water, they were surveyed, and a levee system had to be constructed in order for the water to be somewhat level on the different elevations of the field. I could never understand why they had to be so crooked.

A tractor and a special disc were used to construct the levees before planting. Each levee was then cut with about a 3-4 foot gap for the well water to get to the highest ground. When the low ground area got flooded, the cut would be dammed up in order to fill the next section, and so on and so forth. The cut was filled using a shovel to dig up some of the buck shot mud and place it in the cut area to seal off the water flow.

I can remember one afternoon Bill and I were sealing off some of these levee cuts, and a thunderstorm was approaching quickly. We got in a big hurry. We wanted to complete this project before the storm came. Every time we threw a shovel full of the buck shot mud into the cut, it washed out. We were not gaining any ground. Bill had this idea that if he laid down in the cut, it would slow the water flow down enough so that I could seal it. Guess what? It worked, and we were headed to the house ahead of the thunderstorm.

In the early springtime when there was a lot of rain, Mr. Allison planted his rice seeds using an airplane. This was interesting. There was no GPS system back then. The plane pilot filled the plane's hopper with rice seed and flew out over the field and dropped the seed. Mr. Allison hired me to assist another one of his farm hands to flag for the airplane. We stood out near each end of the field and held up a flag for the airplane pilot to see. When he made his pass over us, rice seed peppered down on our heads. Sometimes this seed would sting a little bit. After the plane passed by, we moved over 21 steps and held the flag up again so the pilot would have a marking as where to fly next in order to get the entire rice field planted. This air rice planting wasn't too bad, and we got paid for it. More money for me!

When we flagged the airplane to fertilize the rice fields or to defoliate the soybeans, things got a little out of hand. Something tells me that we should not have done this. I know that we had to consume a lot of this stuff. I guess it hadn't hurt me, yet. Maybe time will tell. Later in life, I did lose most of my hair, but I think that was hereditary. Maybe, who knows?

When the soybean fields were planted with a tractor, I was given the job of riding on the back of the planter to make sure each one of the planter hoppers was working properly. Sometimes the seed clogged up in the planting tube that extended down from the hopper to the ground. When this happened, I would scream out to Bill, and he would stop the tractor and correct the problem. If this was not corrected immediately, it would leave a skip in the row. We planted four rows at a time. Sometimes my eyes got so tired from watching these seeds that I think they got crossed. Just think that now they can plant 8-12 rows at once. Now that's progress!

Mr. Allison decided to get into the fish raising business. He flooded two 40-acre reservoirs and filled one with catfish and the other with largemouth bass. This was exciting because after the fish grew a little, I got to fish from the banks of these reservoirs and catch just enough fish for us to have to eat. This is where I first learned about bass fishing. These fish were very aggressive and would strike almost anything that you threw into the water. I began to think bass fishing was a piece of cake. Later, I found out that it was an art to out wit these smart fish. At this point in my life is where I got hooked on bass fishing. Mr. Allison didn't want me to catch too many because I would be cutting into his profit.

One day, Bill and I had been fishing over in the Arkansas River, one of our favorite fishing spots, and he had caught a very small flathead -"Appaloosa," catfish. We brought it to Mr. Allison's catfish reservoir and let it go. We didn't know if it would survive or not. But after a few years. when the catfish were harvested, there it was. It had grown into a large catfish and was ready for the dinner table.

A real tragedy struck the bass reservoir when the farmer next door sprayed some of his fields for insects using an airplane; the spray drifted over into the reservoir water and killed most of the bass. What a mess, and the smell was very bad for several months. As luck would have it for me, some of the bass escaped over into some of the rice canals and survived. These bass grew to a fairly large size. When the water flowed through these canals to flood the rice fields, these large bass would suspend right in the middle of the canal by the culvert. They were set to catch their food as it came flowing through. I only had a very few artificial baits. The best one was a "lazy Ike". The bass wore all the paint off it. I soon learned that the bass really liked to feed on worms. I had a couple of plastic worms that didn't last very long before they were chewed to pieces. I then went to work with my forward thinking. There were a lot of worms in the rice fields where the water had created a muddy area. This mud was called "gumbo". I dug the worms out of the gumbo. They were very large and tough. Some would be 10 or 12 inches long. I hadn't heard about the Texas rigged worm for bass fishing, and I don't know when it was invented. But here it was. I put a large hook in the head of the worm without any weight and tossed it out in front of one of these largemouth bass. I had to be careful when I tossed it because it would come off my hook if I wasn't careful. The bass could not stand this, and the fight would be on. What a wonderful experience this was!

I took an old piece of tin that had blown off the barn roof and made me a boat so that I could paddle up and down the farm canals. I could then move around more easily. I didn't like wading through the high Johnson grass on the canal levee. There were many snakes (water moccasins) on these banks. It is a thousand wonders that I didn't get snake bit. I took this old piece of tin and folded it up about a foot on all four sides to make a boat. I covered all the old nail holes to keep the water from seeping through. I used some of the buckshot mud for this. It lasted for a little while, but I had to keep an eye on this because the mud would get wet after a while and pop off. Then the race was on to get to the shore and replace the mud before the boat sank.

One day, my school friend, Bitsy, came over to see my boat. Right off the bat, he wanted to try it out. I warned him to be very careful, for it was not very stable. He would have to stay in the center of the boat when he paddled it. Bitsy was kind of rough, and as he got into the boat, it began to take on water on one side. He tilted it the other way too far, and it began to take on water on the other side. Then, before long, down he and the boat went. This was funny. The water was not very deep, but Bitsy was now all wet. We had to get him dry before he went home. We were pretty good at this. We just rolled him around in the grass for a little while. Then all was good, except my boat was at the bottom of the canal. I think I just left it there for a while. I was getting kind of tired of keeping the nail holes packed with mud, anyway.

Mr. Allison was always very kind to me, and he liked finding odd jobs for me so that I would have a little money for school lunch. It was $1 a week, and if I wanted milk during the afternoon, it was 2 cents for a half-pint box. My mother always seemed to have the lunch money for me somehow. I don't think I ever had to go without school lunch while I was in elementary or Jr. High School. I did without lunch in Senior High School sometimes. I was older and much tougher then. I was becoming bullet proof. I didn't miss the lunch very much because by then basketball had become dominant for me. I played basketball the entire lunch period.

I was now graduating from elementary school into Jr. High School. What a change this would be for me! Instead of being in one classroom all day with one teacher, I was now in a different classroom for each subject, and I had a different teacher for most of the subjects.

The principal, Doyle Burke, was very nice. His wife was also my sixth grade teacher. She was very nice too. He knew my situation at home, and he tried to help me everywhere he could. One day, he came by my house and stopped to talk. I was in the barn digging under some straw to retrieve some earthworms for fishing. When he saw this, he told me that he would like to buy some worms from me. This was great, for there was an upcoming school trip to Oakland Park in Pine Bluff. This would give me a little spending money for this outing. I think Mr. Burke just wanted to make sure that I had some money for the trip. I don't think he ever went fishing. I don't have any idea what he did with his earthworms.

I can remember one time I had a bad day at school. About an hour before lunch, I began to feel a little sick. I told my teacher, and she took one look at me and said that she would get Mr. Burke to take me home. He did just that, and when I got home and ate a few crackers, I got much better. This is the first time that I can ever remember getting sick from being hungry. But that was not the end of my bad day. When I began to feel better, I went outside without my shoes, and as soon as I stepped off the front porch, there it was. I had stepped onto a piece of old rusty wire, and it penetrated my foot. It had to come out quickly. So I jerked it out, and the blood started flowing. I called Momma, and she yelled for someone to get the coal oil. She washed this wound out with soap and water. Then here comes the coal oil. It burned a lot, but it didn't get infected, and I survived. So, I guess this coal oil thing must not have been too bad. Please do not try this at home!

School was great, and I had many friends. One of my best friends lived right down the road. His name was Don Moore. His family had a large cotton farm across from us. Don's parents were really nice to me. Sometimes they would have me over for supper. They had a breakfast menu. They would have sausage and eggs all cooked up together. Boy, was this good!

One of Mr. Moore's farm hands, Adell Lunsford, and Bill became good friends. As a matter of fact, Bill worked with him many years later at the Pickens Farm located near Dumas, AR.

Don had planted a watermelon patch near our house. We got a great idea one day that we would set up a store out near the main gravel road. So, we did this. Don's parents thought this was a great idea, and they told us that we could pick the extra peas that were left in their garden and sell them too.

We got all set up with our store along the road. We made a large sign. It stated that we had watermelon and peas for sale. We even brought a block of ice from the iceman to keep our watermelons ice cold. It didn't take long until we had our first customer. It was a Jackson Cookie vendor. He said he wanted to buy a watermelon. He picked out one and said he wanted to eat it right there, and he would share it with us. Boy, this was the greatest! The only thing wrong was, when he cut the watermelon, it was as green as a gourd, as they say. We cut every melon that we had, and none of them were ripe. The cookie man did buy a bushel of peas. We were very disappointed and out of business.

Don had an old bicycle that he rode everywhere. He even let me ride it sometimes. Some of his relatives gave him a motorcycle. After he got it, he gave me the bicycle. By the time I got it, the left pedal was broken off the holder. I could still ride it, but it was difficult trying to pedal with my left foot pushing on the pedal holder. After pedaling this way for several months, I took it to Mr. Allison's welder and somehow welded a piece of metal out from the holder. I had never welded anything in my life, but I had seen Bill weld many times. I knew enough to use the black glass-welding helmet that protected my eyes from the arc. It certainly was not like a regular pedal that would turn with your foot, but it served the purpose.

Don and I chopped some cotton for his father along with several other workers. I think Don was mostly the water boy, but I chopped right along with all the others. I can remember the heat and those long rows of cotton. We worked ten-hour days for $3.00. What a deal! On payday, we visited a small dry goods store located just down the road. It was not open all of the time. It just opened when a customer showed up. There was a bell that we rang, and the storekeeper would come out of his house next door and open the store for us to shop. He must have been really happy when we would only spend a nickel for a candy bar or a soda.

Don and I had a lot of fun during our limited playtime. We didn't have fun time much, for we had to work most of the time. I remember that we did some fishing in the rice canals. We didn't have any bait, so we would catch grasshoppers and crickets to put on our hooks. The bream or rice slicks liked this bait very well. Also, we found that the worms that were in the ragweed around the barn were excellent bait. We searched for the ragweed that had a big knot on the long stem. We cut into the knot, and there would be a kind of armyworm looking creature. When we found enough of these worms, the fishing would be on!

Louis had been laid off from the river project. He was now working for W.D. Ferguson. He tended the cows and farmed the hayfields. He also planted a couple of acres of watermelons. At harvest time, I helped him, along with Charles and Billy. We picked melons and loaded them onto a trailer so Louis could take them to market. During the growing season, we three were given the job of weeding the melon patch. We knew when the first melon got ripe because every day after they began to get big, we would break one open to see if it had turned red yet. Boy, when they got red, we had a field day. We would just take out the middle and eat it. Louis would say, "I wonder if there are any ripe watermelons, yet?" We could give him the answer very quickly.

Sometimes, during the hot summer months, I would take an extra melon or two with me to work in the hay field. After lunch, we would have a good melon to enjoy. There was one really large guy who must have been the fastest watermelon eater around. We called him Tooto. He was kind of funny. He didn't like for anyone to see him eat his melon, so he would walk behind the truck and eat it. It seemed as though he never stopped walking when he went behind the truck, and when he reappeared, the watermelon was about all gone. Of course, it would be all over his face, but that didn't seem to bother Tooto.

I really liked working in the hay field with the guys. It was very hot and steamy, but I still liked it. It seemed like I was really working and contributing. Bill seemed to like me helping out also. He made a slide to pull behind the hay baler. The hay was compressed in the baler, and two strands of haywire were placed parallel around the bale. I rode on the slide and pulled the bales out of the baler chute and then stacked up 10 bales on the end of the slide. I used a hay hook to grab the bales and assist me in the stacking. I had to wear a long sleeve shirt, no matter how out hot it was because the hay stubbles did a number on my forearms. I then had a heavy metal bar that I used to stick in the ground and use it to slide the stack of hay off into the field. This made it much easier by having a stack of bales, instead of having a single bale at each stop to load onto a truck or trailer.

In the wintertime when we fed the cows, we took a trailer of hay out to the pasture to the hungry, waiting cows. Many of these days were almost unbearable from the bitter cold and wind. As we entered the cow pasture, Bill had a special way to call the cows over to the feeding area. Bill yelled out and here the cows came running. We cut the haywire from around the bales and scattered hay all over the frozen ground. Then the cows had a fantastic breakfast. We did this on many days during the winter months.

Bill was an all around tough guy. The only thing that Bill was afraid of was a spider. After some of the farm hands found this out, they kidded him about this very much. Sometimes they chased him around with a small spider. They loved to see his reaction. Sometimes I think that they didn't even have a spider. They seemed to know when to back off, for Bill would take only so much. Bill was nice to everyone, and everyone seemed to like him. The only time he got mean or wanted to fight was when he drank too much beer or whiskey. He didn't drink very often, but when he did, everyone had to be aware. One time I saw him take his fist and hit a pickup truck tailgate as hard as he could. It dented the tailgate, and it didn't even injure his fist. I think it was a little sore the next day, but he didn't let on. When he was drunk, he seemed to become stronger. One time, I remember he was sitting in Deck's truck, behind the steering wheel with his hands on the wheel. Deck tried to remove his grip from the steering wheel, but he could not budge it. We just had to let him sleep it off.

Sometimes Louis seemed to be a little jealous of me because I was born a little later in life and hadn't had to go through some of the things that he and the others had to go through. Even though I had it plenty rough, I just hadn't had to work as hard as they did. This may have just been in my head, but I got this feeling from time to time. Louis would call me Henry, referring to John Henry for some reason. He would sometimes bully me and maul my head. This action finally got to me. I remember one time I retaliated. When he grabbed my head, I reached up and got a hand full of his black hair. He always combed it straight back, so it was sort of long. I pulled on it very hard. I didn't pull any of it out, but I bet I stretched the roots a little. But this was the end of the head mauling. Bill saw what had happened, and he made me apologize to Louis for my action. I did apologize, but I thought he had it coming to him.

We still didn't have a car. Mr. Allison had an old gray Bell Telephone truck that he used on the farm. He sold it to Bill so that at least we would have some transportation. Bill could not stand the color, so he painted it black. The tires were worn out. They had almost no tread on them. They were so worn that you could almost see the air inside them. Bill replaced a couple of these tires with recap tires. These were very cheap. They were tires that had worn out, and the tire company vulcanized a new set of tread onto them. These worked fine for a while. Sometimes, during the hot summer months, the air in the tires would get between the recap and the old tread and create a large bubble. There was some excitement when these bubbles busted. Recap rubber would fly everywhere. Today, we can see this kind of rubber all over our interstate highways. Most of the freight hauling 18-wheelers use these recap tires. Can you imagine the cost to replace these trucks' tires with 18 new tires? We just need to be real careful not to be along beside one of these trucks when the recap comes loose.

Now, we were moving on up in the world again. I could drive this truck over to Charles and Billy's house and not have to walk the five miles. But, every time I wanted to do this, there was no gas in this truck. So a-walking I would go. I remember that the truck had no signal lights on it - most vehicles back then had none. There were just hand signals. When you wanted to turn left, you rolled down the window and stuck your arm straight out. If you wanted to turn right, you folded your forearm up, and to stop, you held your forearm down.

On one Saturday afternoon, I was at the Allison tractor shed when Bill returned from the soybean field. He was driving what we called a "high boy". This was like a tractor, except it had tall wheels in order to ride above the beans and not injure them while spraying. He raced into the shop yard and turned it too quicklyl It flipped upside down and threw Bill off into the dirt. This could have been another "**Turn in life**" experience for me if Bill had been badly injured or even killed. But, he was fine. He was just shaken up a little bit. He just brushed the dirt off, and we turned the high boy back upright. It was bent up a little, but it was all right.

Louise, Deck, and Barbara came to visit us often. Every Christmas, they brought me a present. Deck was always good to play ball with me. He would hit me some skinners and brag on how good I could catch the ground balls. He said I was going to make someone a good shortstop someday. That made my day. He also let me play like I was a big league pitcher, and he called balls and strikes for me. This was nice. He was about the only adult that would take time to play with me.

Sometimes in the summer, Louise and Deck would let me go home with them and spend a week. They had now moved to Gould, AR. Most of the time, this visit was a lot of fun. I played with my niece, Barbara Ann. She was much younger than me, and she liked to play with those doll things. I was not into that. When I was there on Sunday, Louise took me to the church where she attended there in Gould. Deck had left the farm by now, and he worked for the Gould Zero Gas Company. He delivered propane gas to the farm tanks in the area. Sometimes, I got to go to work with him. This was cool.

After a while, Mrs. Allison invited me to go to Sunday school with them. They went to the Sherrill Methodist Church. I went there almost every Sunday, and when they were out of town, I went with Don Moore and his family. This church was very friendly to me. Several of my school friends went there. Mr. Earl Chadick was my Sunday school teacher. In this Sunday school class is where I learned how to pray and communicate with God. After attending for several months, Brother Bone, the pastor, visited Momma and me. He said several of the kids my age had decided to join the church and be sprinkled on Sunday morning and asked if I would like to be included. I thought about this for a while and decided this was the right thing to do. It would bring me into a much closer relationship with God.

So on that Sunday morning, I was sprinkled and became a member of the Sherrill Methodist Church. Mrs. Allison was excited about this decision. They didn't have any children. I think they kind of took me in for a while. Bill and Momma thought this was good for me, but they didn't talk much about it. The next week, Mrs. Allison took me to Little Rock and bought me some new clothes. She bought me a nice sports jacket and some shirts. I was really proud of these new clothes. I thought that now I could hang with the best of them!

It wasn't long before the Allisons adopted a little girl. She sure was cute. They named her Betty Jane. This must have taken some pressure off of this family growing thing because right after the adoption process, they found out that they were going to have a son of their own. They named him Gordon, Jr. I have heard of this happening to several families when they thought that there would be no children. Then all of a sudden, here came the natural children.

I was doing very well in school. I made A's and B's most of the time. Math was my favorite subject. Mr. Carter was the 7th grade teacher. He was handicapped and walked with crutches. He was a very nice but a stern man. He could get your attention quickly. When he waved one of those crutches your way, you knew that he meant business. His wife had been our 5th grade teacher, and she was very nice.

We rode the school bus every day. This was a long ride from the Allison Farm. I was nearly the first rider to be picked up and the last one to be dropped off in the afternoon. It was about an hour ride, morning and afternoon. I did most of my homework on the school bus. Sherrill School only went through the ninth grade, and then they transferred the students to Altheimer High School by bus. This would be another thirty minutes of bus riding.

Some of the older boys on our school bus begin bullying the Frye boys. This went on for several days, until I got sick and tired of it. It seemed like these boys could not wait for the Frye boys to get on the bus so that they could get started teasing us about something or making fun of how we looked. We were too little to fight them, and the more we complained, the worse it got. So I went to Mr. Burke and told him the situation. I don't know what he did, but the bulling stopped immediately.

Our PE coach, Mr. Thomas, was also one of our teachers. He was a card. He liked to kid us a lot. One day, one of my classmates (Bitsy) and I started cutting up. Mr. Thomas had warned us to stop and to pay attention. Bitsy just kept on going, but I had sensed it was time to stop. The teacher approached Bitsy and told him that he had taken all of this clowning that he was going to take. He got Bitsy by the arm and headed to the office. And when Bitsy passed by my desk, he began to laugh out loud and told the teacher that I was cutting up too. Mr. Thomas was mad by now, so he said, "Frye, you come along too!" Boy, was this bad. He took us to the office, and I thought that he was just going to scold us, but he got out the paddle and told us to bend over. He gave us ten licks each. The first three really hurt, but then the numbness set in, and I didn't feel the other ones. I knew right quick that I never wanted to get in this situation again. What was I to do? I never had a whipping in school before. Now, I had to go home and tell Momma what had happened. She didn't spank me. She just said that if anything like this ever happened again, she would let me have it. I was cool because I knew this was never going to happen again.

Mr. Thomas and I got along a lot better after this incident. I certainly knew better than to push him to his limit. He began to teach us how to play basketball. The playground had a couple of basketball goals with a dirt court. I had a lot of trouble learning about walking with the ball. But, I figured out. If I kept both feet on the ground when I got the ball and then started my dribbling, I could get it done correctly. Mr. Thomas helped us to organize a basketball team. We played a couple of other school in the area. Mostly Linwood and Plum Bayou. We never came close to winning a game, but it was fun and I was learning the game. Later, this would become my favorite sport and pastime.

Another game that most of us boys played was marbles. Most everyone had a few marbles, and during recess, we drew a circle in the dirt that was about three feet in diameter and placed several marbles in the center. They were placed in a straight line at the beginning of the game. Each of us had a special marble which we called "a toy". We then all lagged our toy marbles to a line drawn in the dirt. The closest marble to this line would be the first shooter. We took our toy and placed it near the outside of the circle and then tried to shoot one of the other marbles out of the circle. We shot this toy by placing it in our forefingers and then putting our thumbs behind it so that we could sort of thump it out real fast and strike the other marbles in hopes that one would be knocked one out of the circle.

At the end of the game, everyone got their marbles back. We had some boys in our school who we called "rough necks". These boys always wanted to play keepers. This is where no marbles were given back. We didn't like this game because we would soon lose all of our marbles. These rough necks also started a game they called "grey goose." They would come by and say grey goose, and then they would grab up as many marbles as they could and run away with them. I think this could have been called stealing. This action did cause many fights before our teachers made them quit playing this old grey goose game.

These same "rough neck" boys loved to get creative, especially during our school's Halloween party. One time they got a little carried away and got one of our teacher's chairs and ran it up the flagpole. How they did this, I will never know. It caused quite a stir for a while.

Sometimes at school, we would have a homeroom party. If there were some candy bars, I would make sure I brought one home to Momma because I knew that she never got anything like this. And of course, she would always smile and share it with me.

One day Mr. Monk Bates came into our homeroom class to discuss the cub and boys scout program that was about to begin. They were recruiting for a Sherrill unit. Mr. Bates was very nice, and I already knew him because sometimes he drove our school bus. I got excited about this new program, for it looked like they would be doing some really neat things. They would teach us much about the outdoors and take us on some interesting hikes. I attended a couple of these Boy Scout meetings until I found out the cost involved. I didn't have any money, and if someone did not sponsor me, there would be no way I could do this. You had to buy the uniform or uniforms, pay dues, and the meetings were after school or at night. I would have to hitch a ride with some of my friends. Like I said, I really would have liked to participate in this program. But, as so many things turned out for me during this era of my life, it could be only a dream. I had to forget this and move on.

We also played some softball during recess and at the noon break. We had a make shift softball field out behind the bus maintenance shed. It was right in front of the boy scouts meeting house. Sometimes, the stronger batters would hit the ball off of this house. I can remember one player who could do this consistently. His name was Jim Handley. Jim was head and shoulders above any of us in playing ball. Jim was a very good ball player. His parents took him out of Sherrill School and transferred him to Pine Bluff, which was a much larger school. They felt like Jim had a better chance of making it big time at the Pine Bluff school than he did if he remained at the Sherrill School. I think that this worked well for Jim. The last I heard, he was playing for the New York Mets farm team. Jim played the catcher position. He could throw the ball from behind the batter to second base without ever getting up from his kneeling position. I though that Jim could become a professional baseball player someday.

In our little sandlot ball field, we played the game we called "work up." There were three batters, and everyone else was in the other fielding positions. When one of the batters made an out, he would go to right field and work his way around the positions until he would get to bat again. If someone caught a fly ball, then he would change places with the batter. There were only two bases, first and third. If you made it to first safely, then you got to advance to third, since there were only two more batters.

Right at the end of recess one day, I was trying to catch a pop fly ball, and it happened. This was the only real injury that I had during my school time. I turned my right ankle. The other kids had to help me back to my classroom. The teachers didn't make much of a deal out of this, but it really hurt. When I got home from school that day, my ankle had swollen and turned a little black. Bill and Momma looked at it and made me soak it in some hot Epsom salts water. This helped a little, but that night it got to hurting worse. I thought that I had broken a bone.

I stayed home from school the next day, and Bill took off work for a little while and took me to the doctor. We went to the Altheimer Clinic. The doctor X-rayed it and said that I only had a sprain, and it would be all right in a few days. I guess there was no pain medication back then, for he didn't give me any. He just gave me a pair of crutches and told me to stay off my foot for a couple of weeks.

Well after a couple of days, I was still hurting so badly that now I knew that I had broken a bone, and the doctor was wrong. So back to the doctor we went. He took another X-ray and again he said, "Nothing is broken. It is just a very bad sprain." I guess by now, after a double check, I was feeling better. Anyway, after about a week on these crutches or just as soon as I could hobble on one foot a little, I got rid of those things, and I began to walk again. Today, I still have a bruised looking ankle; but it seems to be fine other than that.

All in all, I didn't have many accidents, just a few scrapes and bruises. One day right at the end of school, several of us boys were playing some sand lot basketball. We were waiting on the Altheimer student transfer bus to arrive. The game got pretty rough. Then it happened. Bitsy's chin hit right on top of someone's head, and after the dust settled, we found that Bitsy had broken off a piece of his front tooth. The other player wasn't hurt much; he just had a headache. I heard Bitsy say, "I don't want to have false teeth." They carried him to the dentist, and they fixed his tooth the best that they could back then. I think he may still have the broken tooth.

At the beginning of the eighth grade, Mr. Burke came to me and asked if I would like to take the Algebra I class with the ninth grade. I don't know why he wanted me to do this, but he said I would like the class and would do fine with it. He said that the eighth grade math would be boring for me. It was like a refresher class of the things that we had already covered, and since I had done well in math, he suggested that I go ahead to the ninth grade class. So, I said yes.

Mr. Burke was the algebra class teacher. He told me to go over to my neighbor's house, and Don Moore would help me to get caught up with the class. He could help me to understand that in this class we would be dealing with x and y instead of all numbers. This was kind of difficult to understand in the beginning, but I caught on pretty fast.

Mr. Burke was a very good and easy teacher. During our test time, he walked around the room from desk to desk, and if he spotted an incorrect answer he would say, "You might want to take another look at that answer." That would mean that the answer was incorrect. He never would tell us the correct answer, but this allowed us another chance to get it correct.

Right before I completed the eighth grade, my mother developed a small growth on the side of her face. It would not heal, so she went to the doctor. He said this was a form of skin cancer. Oh no, my father and now my mother was going to die. What was I to do? We were all scared to death for a couple of days. I think I prayed a lot, even though I don't think I knew much about praying back then.

But, I prayed to God anyway. He must have heard and answered my prayers. The results came back that the skin cancer was benign, and it wouldn't give her any more problems. The doctor was certain that he had removed it all. My mother never had any more problems with cancer the rest of her life.

Chapter 11: The Transfer to Altheimer High School

Altheimer High School

After finishing the eighth grade at Sherrill Barrett, the school rules changed. They decided that they were going to transfer the ninth grade to the Altheimer School. This school was about 30 minutes away by bus. This was not good, and I certainly was not ready to change schools. I had been through this once in the first grade, and it was not good.

I guess maybe there was one good thing. That is, I was transferring with my entire eighth grade class. But at Altheimer, the classes would be much larger, and there would be many more students in each class. I spent the entire summer wondering what this experience was going to be like. I knew that I wanted to try out for the Jr. High Basketball team. I had begun to really like basketball. Momma got me a cheap basketball, and I took the ring from around an old washtub and made me a basketball rim. I constructed a basketball goal, and now I was in business. I played or practiced basketball every day. The cheap ball didn't last very long. It deflated rather quickly, but I just kept playing with it. I couldn't bounce it anymore, but I could still shoot it. It even separated and came to pieces. I still shot it through the hoop. I would watch Jerry West and Hot Rod Hundley from West Virginia on TV, and I tried to simulate some of their moves and shots. I thought I was pretty good, but I was playing by myself with no defense. I had a lot to learn about the real game of basketball, which would become my favorite pastime for many years to come.

So now it was time to go into the ninth grade at my new school, Altheimer High School. Mrs. Lillian Rogers, our English teacher at Sherrill had transferred to Altheimer School and was my English teacher. This was great. I always thought that she was the coolest teacher. I think sometimes she would make eyes at some of us boys. She and her family also attended the Sherrill Methodist

Church. She had a son, Joe, who was a great basketball player for Altheimer. He was the point guard for the senior boys. He and another friend of mine, Buddy Chadick, would do a number on most of the competition in our 8B North basketball league. I always admired these two ball players, and they could do no wrong in my eyes.

The first adversity that I had to face at Altheimer High was, now in the ninth grade, we had to buy our schoolbooks. This was a problem, since I had no money for new books, and I didn't know anyone to buy used books from. Somehow, Bill and Momma dug up enough money to buy some used books that some of my teachers had found from some former students. These books were not very good. They had some torn pages and others were missing. But they would do.

Now, I was headed in the right direction with a whole set of books, I thought. The first week while I was in algebra class, Willie Hooks, our math teacher said exactly what I didn't want to hear. He said we were not going to be using the old algebra book. We are getting new ones. The cost would be $7.50. Now, this was a problem. I did not want to go home and tell Momma that I needed another book. She and Bill had done all that they could do in order for me get the set of used books. This was it. I went home and laid on the couch and played a little sick. Mother left me alone for a while. Then she knew something was wrong and asked me about it. I could not take it anymore. I began to cry and told her that I wanted to quit school and go to work and help her and Bill make us a living.

When Bill got home from work, he told me that he didn't want me to quit school, and he would get the money for this new book from somewhere. I think he borrowed it, but anyway he got it for me. What a good big brother he was to me. I took the money and bought the book, but I knew that this would not be the end of my financial pain during my school time. I still thought about quitting school, but I didn't know where I could find work at this age. This certainly was a "**Turn in Life**." If I had been encouraged to quit school, there is no telling where I would have ended up. God is good!

When I tried out for the Jr. High Basketball team, I made it. I was not on the main string, but I was on the team. This was the best thing since sliced bread for me. I was in high cotton. I was now an Altheimer Red Devil! There at Sherrill, we never won a game. During the ninth grade at Altheimer, we won more games than we lost. Gerald Shepherd was our coach. He was a hard man, and I don't think he ever liked me very much. He never encouraged me very much. He had his favorite few who he catered to. He believed in hard work and discipline. He ran us until our tongues hung out. But this running sure put us in good shape to perform to the best of our ability. I had a lot to learn about the game. I could shoot the ball fairly well, but I had to learn more about defense.

The one thing that I hadn't thought much about was how I was going to get to the ball games, which were located at different schools in the district. Sometimes they would bus us from Altheimer School, but I still had to get to the school to catch the bus. I hated to do this with a passion, but I asked one of my Sherrill teammates to come by and pick me up. They would always do this. Most of the time, their parents would go straight to the game, and I could ride with them. I really felt like I was a burden, but I really wanted to play basketball. Don Moore lived right down the road from me, and most of the time I could ride with him. Freddie Young lived a little farther down the road from Don. Sometimes, I would drive our old truck down there and ride with Freddie and his family. None of these friends ever turned me down, even though I hated to ask them to do this for me. I will be forever thankful for them.

I also liked to play softball, but at Altheimer High School, they didn't play much softball. They played baseball. I made this transition fairly smoothly, and I made the Jr. high baseball team. I played shortstop. Coach Shepherd was also our baseball coach. Same old thing; there was more running. We had a pretty good team, and we would win more games than we lost. The good thing was that I played shortstop, and the varsity team short stop was my friend Joe Rogers. He was a couple of grades ahead of me; therefore, they would need a varsity shortstop by the time I was a junior. I worked very hard for this position, and when the time came, I was awarded with it. I weighed 130 lbs. and was 5'10" tall. I didn't have a real strong throwing arm, but I was quick and could field the grounders really well. The throw didn't matter that much, since my basketball-playing buddy Dub Townsend was playing first base. He had a large first baseman's mitt, and he caught about anything that I threw his way. He made me look good many times. Tim Davis was a good player, and he played 3rd base. He would cut off anything that he could that came our way.

We had a pretty good team. I could hit the ball very well by my senior year. I didn't strike out much at all. I would hit the ball somewhere most all of the time. I would make the other team have to throw me out. I learned my hitting technique from hitting small rocks with an old wooden bat that I had acquired somewhere along the line. I would toss small rocks up into the air and hit them out into a field. I found that the lighter that I held the bat the faster the bat speed would be. This allowed me to hit the ball farther. With this swing, I could pull the ball to the left, which made it go much farther. I took this batting technique over to the real game. If I wanted to hit the ball to the left, I would hold the bat really lightly, and if I wanted to hit the ball to right field or to the right side, I would just squeeze the bat as hard as I could. This slowed the bat speed down, and when the pitcher threw me a fastball, I hit to the right most every time.

Mr. Kirkwood was our Science teacher. He was a very good teacher. He was a different kind of teacher than I was used to. He would ask us to read a book each month and give a book report. I had done this many times at Sherrill, but Mr. Kirkwood was different. He wanted us to schedule a time with him and tell him about the book and answer some questions about it. At first, I didn't know what to expect. I was nervous and had no experience in a one-on-one conversation with a teacher. But I think I did all right. I always got a good grade because I would read the book several times so that I would be able to answer any question that he might have about it. I guess this was called education.

Another thing that Mr. Kirkwood's science class taught me was something that I still use today. It was what he called problem solving using the scientific method. That is: write the problem down and then list several possible solutions. Then begin applying the possible solutions one at a time and collect data to see how each solution would affect the problem. Sooner or later, the problem would be solved or certainly improved. This is a great method that works well for me. I still use it today.

Tim Davis worked with Mr. Kirkwood to create a science project. Tim was very smart and at the top of the class. He created a cloud chamber. It seems that at the beginning of every science class, he and Mr. Kirkwood would discuss his progress on this cloud chamber for several minutes. I don't know what ever happened to this project, but I know that Tim won some awards in several science fairs. Tim went on to become a neurosurgeon. Sadly, I have to say that he passed away this year, 2013.

Now I was moving on to the 10th grade. There was not much excitement going on here, except in our chemistry class. We were preparing science fair projects. I took water (H_2O) and separated it into hydrogen and oxygen. I thought this was a clever idea. Then, for my finale, I took some chlorine and added this to the hydrogen. This made hydrogen chloride (HCL). It is a wonder I hadn't killed someone or myself. I went on to win third place in the fair.

Dub Townsend almost did us all in with his project. His project was to make an aspirin. He didn't get very far along until the mixture that he was heating with his Bunsen burner decided to explode. It didn't hurt anyone, but it liked to have scared all of us to death. It smoked up the area a little bit, and Mr. Kirkwood told Dub to select another safer project and stay away from the medicine making.

So, we all made it through this episode, and as much as I loved to play on the basketball team, I had decided not to try out for the senior high team. Coach Shepherd did not care for me much, and I would not have to worry about trying to hitch a ride to the games. This would be quite a relief for me.

Sonny Davis was the girls' basketball coach, both junior and senior girls. I think he kind of liked me and the way I exerted myself when playing basketball. Sometimes I wished he had been my coach. He said he liked the style of defense that I played.

He was also my American and World History teacher. He was a great guy. Each year, we had to complete a term paper for his class. I remember one year that I choose the history of the mosquito for my term paper. I put a lot research it. It was several pages long, typed, double-spaced. This was ironic, since I didn't know how to type, and I didn't possess a typewriter. Cissi, my niece, had a manual typewriter that she let me borrow. The ribbon was pretty much worn out, but I made do. I typed the term paper with the hunt and peck method, and if I made a mistake on a page, I would retype the entire page. It didn't take me long to be very careful with my typing. About the only thing that I learned from this term paper was that the male mosquito does not bite humans. They feed only on nectar and other juices. I don't think I have ever convinced anyone of this, not even myself. Anyway, Mr. Davis must have really liked my term paper or maybe, he knew how much work I put into it. He gave me an A+. This was the only A+ that I ever received.

Coach Sonny Davis

Coach Davis sometime allowed me to skip study hall and help him with the girls' basketball team. I really enjoyed this. I refereed some of the scrimmages, and I helped out with the warm up drills. This made me think that in the back of my mind I might want to become a basketball coach.

Even though I didn't play on the varsity basketball team this year, I still had a lot of interest in playing basketball. Every day at lunch or during regular physical education class, I played basketball with some of the other boys in my class. I was playing enough during this time that I was getting pretty good. I was even staying in good shape as far as running. Since I had transferred to Altheimer from Sherrill, they would bus us from school to school. When we got on our regular bus route from Sherrill to home, it would be more than an hour's ride for me. The bus made a big loop and my house was at the far end of the loop; however, it would come within a couple of miles of my house at one point of the loop. Whenever the weather permitted, I got off the bus at this two-mile point and ran or jogged most of the way home.

In the fall, I was eager to get home, for there was some excitement waiting for me. Mr. Allison had a blackbird problem in his rice fields during the rice-heading season. This was a few weeks prior to harvest. He had a couple of horses. One was a young filly name Dolly. He let me saddle up Dolly and ride out to the rice fields and shoot off a gun to scare the blackbirds away. I loved this, and I got paid a little. It was a lot of fun until Dolly decided that she had enough of that. She would break for the barn, and I could not stop her. Sometimes she galloped pretty fast, and all I could do was to hang on.

Many times, as soon as I got home from school, I played basketball and practiced until dark. All of this running and practice paid off for me. I really didn't know why I was doing this, other than I enjoyed it. Then one day, the varsity team wanted to challenge us to a scrimmage basketball game. We didn't have a coach, and we had to come up with about 7-8 players. I was elected to be one of those players. Boy, was I excited about this!

The game was set. When we got the ball, I dribbled it down the court for our team. Right off the bat, they gave me some shooting room. I came down and sank a couple of baskets. Coach Shepherd called time out to take care of this issue, for he couldn't let us win the game. He did well, for they shut me down, and they would not let me get any more open shots. We lost the game, but we gave the varsity team all they could handle.

Coach Davis was there at this game, helping out and he still, today, tells me of the time when Buddy Chadick was dribbling the basketball, and I came by and stole the ball from Buddy and headed down court. Coach Davis says that Buddy just looked up and said "Coach, every time I get the ball, someone tries to take it away from me." Coach Davis said he just laughed.

Amazingly, after this game Coach Shepherd told me that I should consider playing for him next year. This was certainly unexpected. I took this as a real honor coming from him. I went out for the team in the 11th grade and made it. I didn't see much playing time in the first part of the year. I guess I had to pay my dues for sitting out in 10th grade.

The only way I got to play much that year was scoring high enough on Coach Shepherd's point system in practice. He had someone to keep data on all good plays or scoring during practice, and the five players with the highest point total for their position would get to start in the next upcoming game. I think, to his surprise, I got the highest score in my position that was graded against a senior starter. I don't think this set well with the player or Coach Shepherd either. But I had earned the starting position according to his rules.

The next game, I was in the starting lineup. After the jump ball, and once down the court, I looked over at the scorer table, and there it was. My replacement was already there to take my place. This wasn't fair. I didn't have enough time to do anything, good or bad. I was not to be out done on this. The very next week, I worked really hard and earned the starting roll again.

This time, I was ready for the exit scene. The tip ball went to me, and I knew that if I didn't go down and get a shot and make it, I was on my way to the pine. As fate would have it, as I rounded the key, a teammate set a screen for me, and I let it go. I had practiced this shot so many times that I could have made it with my eyes closed. Come to think of it, they may have been, for I know I was praying. There was nothing but net, and the game was on. I looked over at the bench, and Coach Shepherd just shook his head. He knew what I had done. But the good thing was, there was no one at the scorer table to replace me. It took about another minute before that happened. But I had proved that I could get it done.

It took several more games before I was taken seriously. I didn't earn the starting position every week, but I became the sixth man on the team and got quite a bit of playing time. I always knew that if I didn't make something happen when I was playing, I would be on the bench quickly.

Coach had a special way to get our attention. When we were practicing to shoot layups, he stood under the goal, and if you missed he would tap you on the rear with a paddle. He never hit us hard enough to hurt anything but our pride. We all tried very hard not to be the one who missed a layup. Think about doing this today, and you would be put under the jail. It didn't hurt a thing; it was just an attention getter.

One time and the only time, we took a road trip to Jonesboro, AR to play a couple of teams located just outside of the city. The teams were Cash and Egypt. I had never heard of either of these two places. Grady High School basketball team went with us on this trip. We all rode on the same bus. This was a lot of fun. One of the Grady players fell asleep somehow on this noisy bus, and one of their players squirted his mouth full of toothpaste. What a mess this was. He came up coughing and spitting toothpaste everywhere.

I think we and Grady ended up winning one game each. We lost to Egypt, but we beat Cash easily. We stayed in a motel in Jonesboro. Some of the boys got pretty rowdy. I remember that the guys next door to Larry Booher's room got really loud. Larry was our team's manager, and he was a very outgoing and exciting person. The boys were shooting craps and rolling the dice up against his wall. They were really loud. When Larry had enough of this, he hit the sheet rock wall with his fist, and it went right through it. Now we were in trouble again. We had to think fast. Larry decided to hang one of the motel room's pictures over this hole. It worked for a while, but after we got back home; they sent him a bill for $50 to fix this hole. He paid it, and life went on.

By my junior year, I began to like it at Altheimer High School very much, even though I had to ride the bus most of the day. One day on the bus ride home, something happened. Fat Robinson was our main bus driver. We didn't know his first name; all we knew was Fat. That is what everyone called him, and he seemed OK with that. He was kind of a large man, and he was very nice. He used discipline when he needed to. He could look through the rearview mirror and give you that look, and you knew that he meant business.

On one occasion a couple of senior boys got into a scuffle, and Fat stopped the bus and made them get off and walk home. Imagine if someone were to do that today. I never heard anything from this incident.

On another occasion, another student, Jerry McKenzie, was pushed against the rear door of the school bus, just as we were beginning to move after letting a student off. The door came open, and out he went headfirst. We yelled and Fat stopped the bus and went around behind it and helped Jerry get up. He had a few gravel scrapes on him. He also had a little blood on the back of his head. Fat brushed him off a little and put him back on the bus. I don't think Jerry ever went to the doctor. Kids were tough back then. If we got a little cut, we would put some dirt on it to stop the bleeding. Please do not try this at home!

Fat Robinson would let one of us stand up front in the door-well and open and close it as students were picked up and dropped off. We all thought this was very cool. One day, Freddie Young was allowed to perform this duty. Fat was following another school bus too closely and when it stopped, Fat didn't have enough time to avoid a collision. He swerved to the left side and swiped the bus, trying to pass it from the outside lane. But there was oncoming traffic and he had to hit the ditch. The ditch wasn't very deep, and we traveled down it quite a ways. When Fat got the bus stopped, it was leaning over so badly that it continued to roll over onto the side. It rolled over very slowly, and no one was hurt. We opened the rear door and exited the bus. It seemed like all of the girls had to step on the windows which were now down by our feet. I think every window was broken. and I don't think any of this happened on the collision.

I had made a lot of new friends here at Altheimer High School, and I liked all of my teachers. Mrs. Wells was my Spanish teacher. She was very nice. I took two years of Spanish, and I made really good grades; however, I never did really learn to speak the language very well. These classes did help me very much, for later in my career, I did some work in Mexico.

Mr. Willie Hooks, our math teacher, liked to fish, and he and I would get together and fish sometimes. On one of our school outings, the group went on a camping trip to Lake Ouachita, near Hot Springs. I remember that we caught a lot of largemouth bass. The water was so clear that you could actually see the fish under the water. We would place our baits right in front them, and they would turn away and not bite. We had to come up with another plan, if we were to catch any of these bass. We decided to back away a little so that they could not see us, and then they began to strike our baits. We were using plastic worms. Mr. Hooks and I also did some fishing together after graduation. He was always fun to be around. He seemed to take things so seriously, and I like to kid around a lot. We got along just fine.

One **"Turn in Life"** thing that I will never forget happened in Mr. Hook's math class. We were studying Trigonometry, and Mr. Hooks gave us a test. I had missed a few days, and I really was not up to speed on what the class had been studying. Trig was very challenging for me anyway. There were so many numbers. Anyway, the test he gave us had five questions worth twenty points each. It took all of the class period to complete. There were several calculations to be made. At the end of class is when it happened. We were to place our test papers on top of Mr. Hook's desk before we left. And then it happened. Satan is everywhere, and he carries very much temptation. BE AWARE!!!

As I laid my test paper on Mr. Hook's desk, there it was. Mr. Hooks had left the answer sheet right on the desk so that anyone could see it. I quickly glanced at it and two of the final answers caught my eye. I took my test paper and corrected these two answers and then laid my test paper on his desk. As I turned to walk away, all I could see were eyeballs of several of my classmates seeing what I had just done. What was I to do now? A very strong lesson can be learned here. God is everywhere, and He is always watching our actions. By the way, as I stated previously, He already knows what we will do in every situation. But he does not dictate that we change it. Our lives can change in a flash.

Whatever I did here was never going to correct my actions. The next day, Mr. Hooks handed us our graded test papers back, and I had made an 80. I only missed one problem. I knew that he only checked the final answers because if he had checked to see how I arrived at my answer, I would have missed the other two problems that I had changed. I knew that I could never change my actions, and also in my mind I would ask myself would I have felt so guilty, if no one had seen me change these answers? God knows everything! This happened just the way he had planned. He had taught me a very valuable lesson.

At the end of this class, Mr. Hooks said that a couple of students that had been absent would be taking this test the next day. I approached Mr. Hooks and handed him my test paper and told him what I had done, and I wanted to retake the test the next day. He didn't say a word; he just looked at me. He never said anything. The next day, he allowed me to take the test again. But, God was not done with me yet. Mr. Hooks gave me the same test problems again. Now, what was I to do? I now know the answers to four of the five problems; all I had to do was to figure out how to get the correct formula. Maybe this was true, but if he didn't grade the formula I used, I may still make an 80, if I only write down the answers. This was not going to happen. I decided it was best for me at this point to go ahead and repeat the two problems that I had gotten correct myself and try to figure out the correct answer on the one that I had legally missed and try and score a 60. This is what I did. He never did discuss this with me. He could have given me a zero or kicked me out of class or a number of things, but he didn't. There it goes to show you that when you try to straighten out a mess that you get yourself into, it gets messier most of the time. One thing that I learned here is that I never wanted to put myself in that position ever again.

So life goes on. Bill had been working very hard for Mr. Allison on his rice and soybean farm. Sometimes during the harvest, I got to drive a tractor that pulled the grain cart. This was used for the combines to empty their grain into, so it could be delivered to the waiting 18-wheel truck. The truck would take the grain to the grain bins. There the farmers would wait for the highest grain price to sell to the market. I loved this job. Mr. Allison bought a Caterpillar to pull the grain cart out in the muddy rice fields. It was almost impossible to get it stuck. I learned to drive it pretty quickly. It had no steering wheel, just steering sticks. You could pull back on one of these sticks and push on the brake on the same side and it would spin around very quickly.

The Caterpillar was not new when Mr. Allison purchased it, and it had some mechanical problems. One was the right side track would come off for no apparent reason. One day, Bill was clearing an old slough area and right before nightfall, when he got right down in the bottom of the slough, the track came off. There was no way to move it until the track was replaced and that would have to wait until tomorrow. That night it rained several inches, and boy this was a mess. The water came up to about the seat on the Caterpillar. We had to leave it there for several days before we could get in there and replace the track. As soon as the water got down low enough, Bill and I had to replace the track and get this thing out of there before it was totally ruined. This turned out to be a major job with the mud and all. Sometimes we just had to guess at what we were doing. You could not see for all the mud. When we finally finished, I think we had about as much mud on us as the Caterpillar had on it. What a mess!

Somehow Bill got hold of enough money to buy him a 1929 Model "A" Ford truck. I think it was antique. The only thing was, it wasn't good enough to be an antique. It was a piece of junk. I think he paid $50 for it. But it would run most of the time. One day, we were using it out in the rice field roads to check some of the fields for water levels. Bill ran off of the dirt road and got stuck. He kept trying to get it out by goosing the gas a little, and he then got both rear wheels in the ditch. There was no way we were going to drive it out of the ditch. Bill had a brainstorm. This old Model "A" truck had a speed throttle located on the side of the steering column. He said that he would set the throttle at about half speed, and we both could get behind the truck and lift it up while we pushed it out.

So here we go. He set the throttle, and the rear wheels began to spin in the mud. We got behind it and pushed as hard as we could push, and out it came. It headed down the dirt road, and we had to chase it down. That was a funny sight to see. The Model A was headed down the road with no driver, and there we were trying to catch it. We caught it before it ran into anything or back in the ditch. So Bill's plan worked, but not just like he had wanted it too.

Bill still was not making very much money, just barely enough for us to get by. He got paid weekly for every day that he would work. During bad weather, sometimes he would work in the shop to repair some of the equipment. This work was only available for a limited time. Mr. Allison suggested that Bill go to Pine Bluff and see if he could find some work in order to help out. Bill found a part time job at the Rose Oil Company. He would work there on the midnight shift. Sometimes I would go with him and help out where I could. Mostly this job consisted of pumping gas into cars. I didn't know it at the time, but this midnight shift work would come back in my later job career.

Once we Frye boys had an idea that we could ride to Pine Bluff with our family as they went to buy groceries on Saturday. We would get them to drop us off at the Oakland Park swimming pool. Then, after swimming for a while, we could walk across town and get a ride home with Bill after he got off from work. On this day, Bill was working the 3:00 p.m. until midnight shift. We boys could help him pump gas, check the oil, and clean windshields at the station when we arrived. Yes, this is what they did to every car that stopped at the gas station back then. What a deal? Sometimes they would even swish out the floorboards.

This was a great idea, and we were excited about it. The walk across town was sort of a long walk, so we decided to take a short cut and not go the smart long way around. This short cut would take us right through a part of town that our parents had told us to stay away from. It was a bad neighborhood. Of course, we didn't understand and certainly didn't listen to them. So here we go.

It wasn't long after we got into this bad neighborhood until a small rock landed right beside us. We turned around, and there were three teen boys about a hundred yards in back of us. Now it was time to be scared. But, we decided to play it cool and act as if nothing had happened, for we had done nothing to cause these boys to harm us. The teenagers got closer and closer, and we could see them very well. This situation seemed that it was going to get a lot worse quickly. They were still throwing some rocks at us.

Now it was time to run. We did just that. We ran fast enough that when we darted around a couple blocks, we lost them or they had decided to move on to another venture. About this time, I looked back and I saw a Police van coming by. I immediately stepped out in the street and stopped it. I told the Police officers all the details of our encounter.

They turned the van around and headed back in the direction of those teenagers, and it wasn't long before they returned. They stopped us and asked us if we could recognize the boys who were in the back of the Police van. Yes we could, for we had gotten a very good look at them. The Police closed the van doors and headed off. I don't think they did anything to these boys, for we filed no police report or anything like that. They probably just rode them around a little while to scare them and then let them go. I really didn't care, for we were all safe from this incident, and we certainly would not be returning to this neighborhood ever again. I guess we needed to pay more attention to our parents. They say you live and learn, and that we did.

Not long after Bill got this service station job, Mr. Allison began a part time job himself. He began to sell insurance. I remember one day he came and talked to Bill about buying some of this insurance for me. He said he would even pay the first couple of months for him. He said he had a great plan, and if Bill paid $50 a month on this plan, that by the time I got ready to retire, I would be rich. I think it was probably an annuity or some kind of mutual fund. The only thing wrong here was that Bill did not have the $50 a month to spare. He barely made this much a month. Needless to say, I had to make it on my own.

When I turned 16, it was time to get my driver's license, and this was quite an experience. Bill had traded cars and gotten an old Buick station wagon. This car was a tank, and it had many miles on it when he got it. There were a few things wrong with it. Bill was a good mechanic and could fix most of the things. There was one thing that he could not fix. It had a fluid speedometer read out, and it was broken. It was kind of neat. It was a green color while you were driving under 60 miles per hour, and above that it would turn a bright red color. Now it was broken and stuck on 100 mph. It was very bright red. Every time you turned the key on, the fluid speedometer would run out to 100 mph and turn red. You never knew how fast you were going. We got used to it not working, and we could tell about how fast that we were going most of the time. There was no way that we were going to spend the money to have this thing fixed. It would have cost a fortune.

Bill let me borrow the old Buick to take my driver's test. I drove to the Pine Bluff Courthouse and took my written test. I had studied the driver's pamphlet and had no problem passing this part of the test. Now, I was to take the test-driving part. I will never forget this incident. The trooper walked me to the car and got into the passenger seat. I started the old Buick and here we go. The old fluid speedometer moved from green to bright red, and we hadn't even moved yet.

The trooper said, "Whoa, what's up with that?" I said, "It's broken, but we will be fine."

He said, "No we won't because I cannot give you the test in this vehicle until that thing is fixed."

He had to know that I had driven myself up to the courthouse because there was no one there with me. I thought for a minute, and I asked the trooper if I got another car, could he still give me the test today?

He said, "Yes." And I said, "OK, I will be right back." I was smart enough to wait for him to go back in the courthouse before I drove off.

I went straight to the Sunbeam Bread Company and borrowed Buddy's car. It was an old green 4-door Chevrolet. So I drove back to the courthouse and told the trooper that I had another car, and I was ready to go. After a while, he came out and got in. We were just about ready to go and he said, "I need to check your headlights." *Now, why in the world would he have to do this?* I will never know. Anyway, he tried to open the passenger side door, and he couldn't get out. I told him to just roll down the window and he could open it from the outside. He looked at me with a little smirk on his face and said, "Sorry, young man. You cannot take your driver's test in this car, either." Man!! *What was I to do?* I was about to run out of options.

After he went back into the courthouse, I went around the block and took the door handle off the back door and put it on the passenger side door. It now worked great, but now there was no back door handle. So, here I go again, back to the courthouse for the third try. By this time, I think the trooper was getting a little frustrated with me. He got in, and here we go. He didn't check the back door to see if it would open from the inside. He just had me to drive around the block and back to the courthouse and park. I guess he figured that I could drive, since I had driven all over town that day. He said, "Congratulations, young man. You passed your driver's test, and you can now get your driver's license." I bet he remembered me for a while, but I had my driver's license.

After I got my license, Bill let me drive the old Buick to school when we had a late basketball practice. I used this as a payback for some of my teammates for taking me to the games so many times. One day, I picked up Bitsy Chadick and let him ride with me. He lived a little ways up the road from me. So I would have to drive a couple of miles past my road to take him home. Bill had told me to be careful, for the brakes on the old Buick had been giving him some problems. Boy, was this ever true! There were no brakes! I had to use the emergency brake every time I had to stop. I think this made Bitsy a little nervous. I would slow down and slowly pull on the emergency brake cable. We would come to a slow stop and not slide the wheels. Of course, I had to learn this by trial and error. The first few times we had to stop were quite an experience. I would tell Bitsy, "Hold on, man!"

My next automobile experience came right after Bill traded this old Buick for a smaller car. It was a Ford Falcon. It was much more economical. I was driving this car to the next basketball game at Altheimer. I had picked up some of my friends who had been giving me rides to the games. They were Louis and Ray Clinton. On this night, the fog had set in pretty heavy, and of course, it was dark, and you could only see a few feet in front of the car. I was very careful and was driving very slowly. I came to a stop sign near Altheimer. There was another car behind me, and they stopped also. I began to move out into the road, and I could not see if the road was really clear, so I stopped again. Then it happened. The driver of the car behind me thought that I had gone on out into the highway, and he hit me from behind. Louis was sitting in the back seat when the jolt hit. He yelled out, and this scared me, for I was thinking the worst. This was my first wreck. We got out and surveyed the damage, and there was none. It looked as if our bumpers had matched, and it hadn't bent or broken anything. Louis did have a bump on his head, and he said it hurt. We just told Louis to suck it up, and he would be all right. So on to the ball game we went. I don't think I played very well that night. I had to tell Bill about this incident. He didn't take it too badly. He just said that I would have to be a little more careful.

There was another time this old car just quit running on me. I didn't know what to do. I had a couple of my friends in the car with me. I was embarrassed because this old junky car had quit running, and their families all had nice cars that would run. I had to do something, fast. I raised the hood to take a look. I had seen Bill work on all kinds of automobiles and tractors for some time now. Therefore, I had a little experience in mechanics.

After looking at most of the things that I thought that could be wrong, I stood back and assessed the situation. Now this thing had to have gas and battery current to run. It had some gas in it, so that was not the problem. Remember the scientific solution to problem solving that we discussed earlier? Here it is in action. Next I took a look at the battery current. The battery was fine, and all of the connections were fine. Next, was to trace the battery current as far as I could. Everything appeared, OK. But, when I took off the distributer cap, there it was. A broken distributer wire was the culprit. I twisted both ends of this wire back together, and the car started and ran fine. What a deal this was for me! I had repaired my first automobile, and we were off again.

In my junior year, it was time to buy our class rings. I knew that this was not going to be possible for me, for there was no money. My dear mother made this dream comes true for me. She had saved one of her welfare checks and gave this to me so that I could buy the class ring. That was a great big surprise for me. I will never forget that precious moment in my life when she gave me this money. I really didn't want to take it because I knew she could not afford it. She said she wanted me to have this ring, and I was to get it. Thank you very much, Mother.

Chapter 12: My Senior Year of High School

I really had a scare right before basketball season. Coach Shepherd told us that some of the rules had changed, and we were now required to get a physical before we were allowed to play on the basketball team. I thought his would be no problem, except the hassle and cost to have it done. So I got Bill and Momma to take me to the doctor for this checkup. They carried me to mother's doctor, who was Dr. Talbot in Pine Bluff.

He checked me over and said that I would have to come back the next week before he could release me to play basketball because my blood pressure was very high for my age. What was this? I wasn't having any physical problems. I felt fine. I told Coach Shepherd about this, and he said not to worry about it. He assured me that I would be fine and that I would get to play. That made me feel much better, but I didn't know how to take this.

I went back to the doctor the next week, and he said that my blood pressure was still a little too high, and I would need to keep a check on this, but he was going to give me a release to play basketball. Boy, was this good news! This blood pressure thing never bothered me during the season, but it went on to give me some problems for the rest of my life. Later, I would have to take medicine to keep it under control.

During my senior year, basketball was about all that I could think about. I couldn't wait for basketball season to begin.

I called Coach Shepherd on a couple of occasions during the summer, and he would come over and open the gym up for me, and I would shoot the basketball for several hours. This was fun, and I think it helped me to improve my shooting skills. However, being in an actual game was much different than practice. You had to adjust to the crowd, which in the beginning, was difficult for me. It made me very nervous. I found that if I just ignored the crowd, I could play much better. The only problem was when I would tune the crowd out, I would also cut out the coaches. Coach Shepherd would shout pretty loud and had a special way to get your attention. Sometimes it would be too late, for I had already blown it.

Coach Shepherd was a very good coach, and I liked him very much, certainly more than he liked me, or so it seemed. He had some strict rules that we players had to abide by. During basketball season, we were to have no Cokes or candy bars. These rules were not very hard for me to follow, since I didn't have any of these things anyway. Of course, he didn't allow any of us to smoke. I know that some of the players did smoke, and even at this young age, you could tell that it was affecting their breathing capacity. We had one player who would try to skip some of the running laps around the gym floor. When Coach Shepherd wasn't looking, he would dart into the dressing room. I think he got caught every time. Then Coach Shepherd made him run additional laps.

One time, right after basketball practice, something pretty strange happened. As we ran across the gym floor to our dressing room, we would see how high we could jump and try to touch the basketball goal rim located on the far end of the court. The gym had just had a makeover. They had installed new fiberglass backboards and painted a huge red devil (which was our mascot) in the center of the court. I could barely touch the basketball rim with my highest jump. Dub Townsend, being a little taller, could get his hand onto the rim. On this day, he did his best jump and got a hold of the rim. There was no break away rim. He hung on a little too long, and the glass backboard shattered. It looked like it was in slow motion. It shattered and then began to fall down on the gym floor piece by piece. What a mess!

They had to go out on the tennis court and get one of the old metal backboards and put it back up here because we had a basketball jamboree scheduled the next weekend. We were to play four different teams so that the fans could get a look at who had what. We played a half of a game with each team.

I remember that right at half time of the first game, I had the ball just past the half court line. I put up a very lucky shot right after hearing the buzzer sound. It hit right off the backboard and went through the rim. The fans went wild. Right after the game, Kathryn (Kitten) Albright, a fellow student who had been in my classes since first grade, came up to me and said that she had a feeling that I was going to do something special tonight. I said, "Kitten, it didn't count. The shot was after the buzzer." She said she didn't care. It was still a great shot. This made me feel really special that she would make this comment. Kitten was always a very nice girl. She was very talented. Many times during our class plays or assemblies, she would tap dance for our group. She was very good at this.

I was not much of a rebounder, so I had to find something else I could do to help our team. It took me a while to understand the real deal about the coaches. They were not there trying to teach us basketball. They were there to keep us under control and organized. We had to learn how to perform the best way that we could. I worked extremely hard on my defense and got pretty good at it.

I found that, as the opposing team would bring the ball down the court into our waiting defense, I would watch the ball handler's eyes. I noticed one thing that helped me on defense. Especially with the better ball handlers, they would always look at their receiver and then look away while they threw the ball to this player. Well, I figured that out pretty well. I would bait them to come my way, for I would back away from the player I was guarding to give the ball handler an easy read to throw the ball my way. And then when he looked away to set up his fake pass, I would dart in front of the player. Sometimes, I would make this ball handler look pretty bad because it looked like he threw it straight to me. Of course, since I was playing the front guard position, I would usually have a straight run at our goal on the other end of the court for an easy layup.

Right after I began doing this, our players on the bench started to call me Casper, after the friendly ghost. Some of them said I was so skinny that if I would turn sideways and stick out my tongue, I would look like a zipper, ha ha.

Another thing I started doing on defense was to cut the man I was guarding out of the game. I would guard him so closely without the ball that his other teammates could not pass it to him. Boy, did this cause some frustration on their part. How could they score any points if they didn't get the ball? That's the way I saw it too.

Coach Shepherd finally picked up on this type defense and would assign me the best player of the opposing team to guard. My job was to keep him from getting the ball. I remember how this came back to haunt me in a game against Grady. We were one point ahead with only seconds to go in the game. I was guarding James Truitt, their best shooter. I had held him to only a few points, and he had gotten very frustrated. Late in the game, I had gotten into foul trouble and had to back off a little. With only seconds to go, Grady inbounded the ball quickly. I had given up, for I knew that they did not have time to go down court and get any kind of decent shot. I could not locate James Truitt until it was too late. I looked up, and he had the ball, and I could not get to him. As you know, he let it go from nearly half court and made the bucket to win the game. I felt about as bad as I could have felt because this was my fault. I took it like a man, but I didn't like it at all. I went into the Grady dressing room and congratulated the team on the win. They were really celebrating and shouting. This was a great win for their team because we had beaten them easily at our place.

Another game that I can remember was against Humphrey. They were out to beat us badly. The game started kind of slow, but we had built a pretty good lead. They began to get really aggressive. Each time we would set up a screen for our players, they would pinch us in the ribs. We told Coach Shepherd about this, and he informed the referees. They never caught them in the act. I'll never forget right before half time as I was guarding one of their players very closely. He stepped right on the out of bounds line. The referee was standing right there. I got excited and asked the referee if he didn't see this. The referee acted as if he hadn't heard me. I grabbed him by the arm, just to get his attention. Boy, did I get his attention. He blew his whistle right at me, with a technical foul. I didn't mean any harm. I just wanted him to answer my question. This would be my one and only technical foul.

By the third quarter, we had gotten way ahead of Humphrey, and both coaches were getting into shouting matches. The Humphrey coach called it quits, and they left the game before the end of the third quarter. The final score was 57-42. I was having one of my better scoring games, and I didn't want them to stop the game early. I had scored 17 points with another quarter left to play. What a shame.

Right after the game, I was very impressed with Coach Shepherd. He told me to go find the referee and apologize to him. I did just that. His name was Mr. Bailey. He was very polite and thanked me for my apology. The next game that we had with him refereeing, he came up to me. He said that he had an extra whistle with him if I thought that he might need some help. I told him that I didn't want any part of that. I thought that he would do just fine. After that we became good friends.

We basically had one offensive play. We ran this until it broke down, and then we were on our own. Every player had a route to take during this play. However, Jimmy Moore, our point guard would bring the ball down the court, and the other two guards would set up a screen for him. Many times this is as far as we would get for Jimmy would shoot off this screen, and he was pretty good. He would score most of the time. But, when the opposing coaches picked up on this play and shut him down, it was someone else's turn to take over.

I found that I could break this play down pretty quickly and do about what I wanted to do then. I don't think coach Shepherd ever really knew that I would break the play down on purpose. My plan was to keep moving and break to the ball as quickly as I could, and if I was open, I would fire a shot. I used my earlier experience quickly in every game. I would take a couple of shots early, and if I would make some of them, then I would continue to throw them up until I began to miss a few. This process worked well for me because I probably shot a couple hundred shots every day in practice, at home, and during lunch.

Once we played a team that I had never heard of before. It was Vilonia, located near Conway, AR. The day before the game, the starting lineup was asked to give some comments during our school's open assembly. When it came my turn, I really couldn't think of anything to say. So, I asked everyone to bring plenty of sliced bread to the game, for we were going to be slicing up a lot of bologna tonight.

This statement came back to haunt me. For this was the worst scoring game for me during my senior year. I couldn't hit the broad side of a barn. I scored a total of 3 points. I remember the only basket that I made was a very long one. I was right near our bench and probably out of scoring range, and I shot it. It went in, and I breathed a sigh of relief. At last I had scored. We got beaten 49-63. What a game for me. I just could not get on the right track.

I learned that to be really good at shooting the basketball, you had to be in a zone in your mind. Most of time, I found myself just shooting the ball at the hoop and hoping that it would go in. But when I could get into that zone, I found that it became very easy to score. Of course, to get in this zone, I would have to tune everyone out, including the coaches. I had to trick my mind into thinking that I could make every shot. I found that I could not make the ball go in the basket. I could force it up close and hit the rim or backboard most anytime, but it would not go in. It would just rim out. But, when I was in the zone, I would go up for a jump shot or layup and make up my mind that it was going in the goal, and then my subconscious would tell my muscles how to react to make this happen. You cannot do this on purpose. Things happen too quickly for you to tell your muscles what to do. You just have to relax and let it happen. I have used this process for many other things. I just wish I had better control of this action because it works.

I have been in this zone with my Lord on a few occasions. When this happens, it is just as you have some unknown peace of mind, knowing that everything is going to be all right. I guess, God may be showing us a little bit of heaven. When this occurs, all of the pieces of life's puzzle seem to fit together perfectly. Nothing else matters. God is good. But when we realize that we can fail, we usually do just that. Self seems to get in the way of our faith.

Matthew 14:29

And he said, Come. And when Peter was come down out of the ship, he walked on the water, to go to Jesus.

This is real faith or getting into the zone of God. But, we must have the faith that we can continue, or we will fail.

Matthew 14:30, 31

But when he saw the wind boisterous, he was afraid; and beginning to sink, he cried, saying, Lord, save me.

And immediately Jesus stretched forth his hand, and caught him, and saying unto him. O thou of little faith, wherefore didst thou doubt?

I only wish that I could muster up enough faith to stay in this zone forever.

Whenever I would get the chance, I would like to slip over to the baseline corner and shoot. This was my favorite place to shoot. I would not miss many from this area. My senior year, I averaged 15 points per game. I remember the Jefferson County tournament played at Humphrey, AR. One night, we were playing Wabbaseka, AR. Before the game, one of their players came up to me and said that their coach had told him that he would be guarding me all night. He needed to shut me down. Their plan didn't work. I don't even remember seeing him on the court that night. This statement must have turned me on, for I scored a career high 35 points that night, and our team posted 98 total points. They were never in the game. Everything I shot that night seemed to find the basket. Even at that, I had to set out most of the second quarter because of foul trouble. I only scored 2 points in this quarter, but I turned it on again in the second half. Toward the end of the game, Coach Shepherd called time out and told the rest of the team to feed me the ball and let me run my score on up.

He said he thought I already had about 100 points, and he wanted to see if I could score more.

The team began to get the ball to me more; however, by this time, most of the other team was guarding me, and I barely could get a shot off. I remember the last shot to score 100 points total, which we had never even come close to before. Dub Townsend got the rebound and headed to the other end of the court. Just over half court, he let the final shot fly. He almost made it for our 100th point. It just fell off the rim. Oh, how I wish I could have got my hands on that ball before the buzzer sounded. But to no avail, we had to settle for 98.

All was not lost. We won the Jefferson County Tournament, and I was selected as the most valuable player. This was the highlight of my basketball career. What a night! I will never forget it, even though I would go on to play some degree of basketball for several more years.

We had a winning season; however, we lost in the finals at the District Tournament to Woodlawn by 2 points. This was a heart breaker. We really wanted to go to the State Tournament in Little Rock's Barton Coliseum. Coach Shepherd did take us there to watch Woodlawn play. They got beaten in their first game by Lake Hamilton from Hot Springs. This team had beaten us badly earlier in the year.

1963 ALTHEIMER SENIOR RED DEVILS

(Left to Right) Billy Bryant, Danny Murdock, Harold Anderson, Jerry Bost, Charles Chadick, William Givens, Ray Clinton, Johnny Frye, Stan Townsend, Don Rainey, Jimmy Moore, Dub Townsend, Tim Davis, Ricky Webb, Jim Duck, mgr.

RED DEVILS SPORTS SCOREBOARD

Basketball

Altheimer	79	Kingsland	53	18
Altheimer	73	Glendale	87	18
Altheimer	49	Vilonia	83	3
Altheimer	57	Humphrey	42	17
Altheimer	59	Wabbaseka	28	17
Altheimer	88	Grady	89	11
Altheimer	47	Lake Hamilton	68	6
Altheimer	62	Glendale	71	10
Altheimer	65	New Edinburg	42	10
Altheimer	76	Wabbaseka	55	15
Altheimer	86	Kingsland	53	21
Altheimer	71	Humphrey	47	10
Altheimer	62	Woodlawn	57	17
Altheimer	86	Plum Bayou	44	13
Altheimer	52	Grady	54	16
Altheimer	99	Wabbaseka	64	35
Altheimer	78	New Edinburg	09	12
Altheimer	81	Grady	68	11
Altheimer	57	Woodlawn	69	10

1963

262

"This team was a fine bunch of boys to work with. They missed going to the State Tournament by only two points. Even though we lost eight good players from the 1962 team, we worked hard and came back strong. I'm as proud of this team as any team I've ever coached."

COACH GERALD SHEPHERD

During the Altheimer's Honors Day ceremony, I got a big surprise. Every year, the best all-around basketball player would be elected to the Altheimer Hall of Fame. There had always been only one player allowed per year. But this year was different. The selection committee changed the rules, and when the names were announced, they called out Jimmy Moore, Dub Townsend, and Johnny Frye. What an experience for me! All of that hard work had finally paid off. We each received a small trophy. I think I still have it today. It wasn't worth much, but it was like gold to me.

Each year, there was a basketball game between the hall of fame players and the senior high team. This was a lot of fun. This went on for several years, but after a while, things began to change drastically in the educational process. There is no longer an Altheimer Hall of Fame. There is not even an Altheimer High School. Consolidation took over, and all of the smaller schools closed down. What a shame! There was a lot of history and memories made at these schools. Kids today will never realize what they will miss in their lives by not being able to attend one of these small schools.

Our senior class was taken all the way to Hot Springs, AR for our senior trip. We were there for a couple of days. I think this was quite an experience for some in my class. I think some of them had more fun than they should have.

On one of the days that we were there, Larry Booher rented a speedboat for a half day. Larry had polio and had to wear a brace on his legs. This was very restricting for him. He could walk, but with limited mobility. Since all that Larry could do was to drive this boat, he invited me to go water skiing. Of course I didn't know how to water-ski. Anyway, after many spills, I learned how to ski, and he pulled me all over Lake Hamilton.

Boy, did I get too much sun! The next couple of days, I was miserable. All in all, we had a great time. We all had gotten one of those lifetime experiences.

Larry was a very outgoing person, even with the polio, and he was a great friend of mind. We got along great together. Many times at lunch, Larry would go to the corner store, which was located right up the street from the school. Many of the students went there for lunch. At least, the classmates who had some lunch money. They had great fast food. They also had a couple pinball machines. I remember that I would go there just to watch Larry play these machines. He would go wild and shake these machines around until they would show tilt on the screen. Then he would put in another nickel, and here we would go again. This was a lot of fun for Larry, and I really enjoyed watching him play these games.

On Friday nights, many of the boys in our school who had fast fancy cars would meet somewhere and drag race. They would locate a favorite stretch of highway that was very straight. Then they marked off a ¼ of a mile stretch and paired off with a car in each lane of the highway, both facing the same direction. And here they would go, just hoping that there would be no oncoming traffic that needed to use the outside lane. This was very exciting and very illegal. I think the local police knew about this because the tires would leave several black streaks on the pavement from the burn out. They didn't care, as long as it didn't cause anybody any harm. It was a really cool thing for the one who had the fastest and the loudest car in high school. Most of the cars had a modified muffler called a "glass pact." These cars sounded as if there was no muffler at all. If the police caught anyone showing out or abusing someone with these noisy pipes, they would issue a warning citation. Then they would tell them to remove the glass pact muffler, ASAP. I didn't have access to any car that I could use for this activity. I always wanted to do this, and later in life I got my opportunity. We will cover this later in my next book.

During the spring of my senior year, I began to work on the farm more and more. Bill was now working for George Davis. Mr. Davis was a very fair man. We were allowed to move into one of Mr. Davis's farmhouses. This house was certainly a move up for us. It had plumbing with hot and cold running water. We could now use the bathroom indoors. This was a first for us. The house was good for us. The only thing wrong here was there were many rats around. They were in the attic and the walls. I don't think there was any insulation in the house. During the night, they would get started. You could hear them clawing in the walls and the attic. I don't think any of the rats ever got into bed with me, but they were plenty annoying. One time, they descended into our kitchen, and we chased rats for a while. I remember they ran under our cook stove. I don't think we ever caught one. They were huge. They seemed to be nearly as big as a cat. We had a pig in a pen just outside by the shed, and I guess this is what attracted the rats. I think the rats grew so huge from eating on the corn that we used to fatten the hog.

When I worked for Mr. Davis, I would drive a tractor to get the fields ready for planting. He paid me $7.50 a day. This was the same thing that he was paying all of his tractor drivers. I thought that I had finally grown up. This work was not very difficult for me because all you had to do was just sit there and drive the tractor. It was very dirty work, for there was no enclosed cab for the driver. You just had to breathe in all of that dust. At the end of the day, I would be covered from head to toe with dust.

Of course, I was missing a lot of school for this tractor driving work, and this was affecting my grades. They had begun to slip a little. Was college to be in my future? I couldn't see it. So many things had to line up for this to happen. How could I even get there? How could I afford it? Where would I go? How do I apply? Would I be able to play on the college basketball team? I needed a plan. I didn't know where to start.

My sliding grades were a real bummer to me. I was used to making A's and B's. During the last semester of my senior year, we were informed that we would become a part of the National Honor Society. The only problem for me was that you had to have at least a B average. This was very disappointing for me. I found out that my grade average had slipped to a C+. I was just a few points shy of the standard B. I could not believe I had done this. If I had only known that this honor was coming, I could have easily made it. I had found that skipping school and working was not that important. But it was what it was, and there was nothing I could do about it. My life was changing, and I would have to stand up and make some very harsh decisions.

Mr. Hooks told us something one day in class that I had never really thought much about. He said that he knew that all of us had become very close friends, kind of like a family. But we were very near graduation, and chances were that we might never see each other ever again. This was so true. After graduation, there were a few reunions held, but not everyone attended. I never attended one until 2010. We graduated in 1963. That is 47 years. I have seen a few of my fellow students out and about, but not many. Most of them I never saw until this 2010 reunion, and several of them did not even attend this reunion.

Here are some of my favorite classmates. Jimmy Moore and I played some independent baseball right after high school, but since I have lost contact with him. J.D. Craig and I played some independent basketball for a few years after high school. We had some great times together. Alta Young has retired to Hot Springs. I still stay in touch with her via e-mail. Delores Wardlaw retired from teaching, and I stay in touch with her via Facebook. I can remember that she asked me to be her campaign manager in high school to help her get elected to class representative. I was very happy that she won the election. In our open assembly, I gave a campaign speech and stated that "Whether it was dry cleaning clothes or being a junior class representative, you could not go wrong with a Wardlaw." Her dad, Herbert, ran the local dry cleaning business. He was also an avid basketball and baseball fan.

Jane Couch is still working at a Christian Literature Supply Company in Texarkana, AR. She is near retirement. My wife and I visit with her from time to time. We are still great friends, and she is a sweet lady. Another great friend of mine from high school that I haven't seen since graduation is Dub Townsend. I hear that he went into the funeral business. It seems that Mr. Hooks had gotten it right. Many of us would never, or hardly ever, see one another again.

I understand that several of my high school friends married their high school sweet hearts. Charles (Bitsy) Chadick and Wilda Bryant; Maxine Pipkin and Jerry Bost; Judy Moore and Don Fox; Judy Robinson and Jerry Clem. All retired to Hot Springs. Others that I know of were J.D. Craig and Brenda Gossage; Harold Bradley and Marie

Stokes; Larry Scoles and Sylvia Stacks; Eddie Everett and Judy Grisham; Barbara Bolin and Todd Davis (both are deceased). This is more than I had dreamed that would stay together from Altheimer High School. These were all great friends of mine in school and still are today. I just do not to see them very often.

Jung Mae Lee and Jimmy Fowler were also very good friends of mine. Jung Mae's parents had a store located there in Altheimer. Jimmy's mother was the fourth grade school teacher at Sherrill, and his father was our mail carrier. Both of these boys loved to play Ping-Pong, especially when the weather was bad, and we couldn't go outside during recess. Both were very good players, and I could never beat them, but I tried many times. Jung Mae also played tennis very well, and I would challenge him to a match on occasion, but I could never beat him at this game either. So I just stuck to playing basketball and baseball.

In my second semester, I met with our guidance counselor, Mrs. Walker. She was a great lady, and she helped me a great deal. She set me up an interview with the decision making board of the large farm owner in the area, Elm's Plantation. They offered a scholarship to the most deserving and needy senior student each year who wanted to continue his education. This scholarship was very good. It paid $500 a semester as long as the student remained in school.

The interview went well. I certainly could explain the need and the desire to go to college. Most of these board members were huge Altheimer basketball fans; therefore, they all knew me very well. Anyway, I got the scholarship with one little wrinkle. It was given to two people, me, and another classmate, Gary Williams. We were to split it. Each would get $250 a semester. I think Gary's parents were working for the Elm's Plantation at that time, so it made a lot of sense that he would receive one of these scholarships.

This was still good for me, but not what I had hoped for. But, this would weigh greatly on my final decision. Also, Mrs. Walker had me to fill out an application for the Arkansas State Teachers' Scholarship. I had told her that my ambition in life would be to go to college and become a coach. Of course, back then there were no full time coaches. They had to also teach a class or two.

In a couple of weeks, I was informed that I had received this State Teachers' Scholarship. It was a one-time payment of $100. Now, I was on a roll and had to make up my mind on where I was going to college. Charles Batson, a close friend and classmate of mine said he was going to visit Southern State College located in Magnolia, Arkansas, and I was welcome to ride with him and his family on the visit. I agreed.

We visited the college, and Charles seemed to like it very well. Later, he did attend here. I was OK with the college;

however, I was still not very comfortable with this college thing. The one thing that would have made a large difference was basketball. I checked to see if there may be a basketball scholarship available. I was informed that all of the full scholarships had been given out, and I was welcome to come here and try to make the team as a walk on. This would be a piece of cake for me. I just knew that I could work hard enough to make this happen, but I would have a lot on my mind, and I would be away from home for the first time ever. Also, the grades would have to be good.

As time went on, Charles and I became much better friends. His parents had an old Nash Rambler for their family automobile. It was really small. He and I doubled date a few times with our girlfriends. He had a girlfriend, Dianne Coverdill, but I didn't have a girlfriend. Cissi, my niece, said that one of her friends would like to go out with me. Her name was Pam Pipkin. She was much younger than me.

I asked her out, and she said yes. So this was my first date. We double dated with Charles and Dianne. We took his Nash Rambler and drove to Pine Bluff, and we drove around where all of the kids hung out and then back home. Pam was too young for me and that was our only date. I don't know where she ended up or where she went to college.

Now, it was time for the senior prom. Tim Davis said that Betty Kirkpatrick wanted me to ask her to the prom. She was a senior and was in some of my classes. She had a twin sister, Bonnie. I asked her if she would go with me, and she said yes. Here we go back to Charles Batson and the Rambler and another double date. The prom was fun, and after the prom we drove to Pine Bluff. Charles thought that it might be fun and scary if we would drive by an old palm reader's house and see what was happening. I think he had heard about some of the other kids doing this and seeing some strange things occurring.

We did drive by the house, but we didn't see anything. I think we made up some scary stuff in order to scare the girls. It must have worked, for both of the girls said they wanted to leave. It looked too scary.

Betty and I dated for the rest of the school year. We never went steady or anything, but I think she liked me very much. I was not ready for this girl thing. There were too many other things going on in my life to get serious about a girl. I did not treat Betty fairly at all. For after graduation, I got so involved in the things that got balled up in my life that I didn't have any contact with her for a long time. Then, after a while, I had heard that she had begun dating somebody else, and that was fine with me. I never saw or spoke with Betty again. Sadly, I just heard that she passed away this year, 2013.

Chapter 13: The Last Chapter

I still remember that we had a special program right before graduation night. I was one of the lead characters in this program, and our English teacher, Mrs. Lillian Rogers, directed it. I was a scarecrow. Maybe I got this role because I was the only person who looked like a scarecrow. The song that we sang was so true, and I still believe in it today. That song was "We are Forever Blowing Bubbles. They fly So High and They Fade and Die." What a parallel to life this is.

Bill and Momma attended my high school graduation. This was a real honor for me, since I was the only one in my family who was allowed to accomplish this feat. It wasn't easy, but I got her done. Bill really sacrificed very much so that I could finish high school. I am so thankful for him. This was about the only time that they ever attended any of my school functions. They did go to one of my basketball games during my senior year. It was against Plum Bayou. We won the game, and I scored about 15 points. They didn't seem to care. They always supported me to stay in school, but that was about it. They didn't seem too excited about the whole thing. It is amazing that I completed this task.

Louis and Nadine also attended our graduation ceremony to see Charles and Billy graduate. What a deal. The Frye boys had done it together. The Frye factor was about to hit the world. Look out world!

God is good. He placed us here on earth to spread His good Word by our words and our actions. This is not very complicated to figure out. Just read His Word, and He will speak to us, and we can talk to Him through our prayers. I think many times we humans get things so complicated that we don't know what to do next. We don't need to get ahead of God. We need to have patience. Many times, we get excited and think that we have it all together, but let's not fool ourselves, God is still in control, and we need to seek his direction for our lives and mature in is faith as we grow older.

This is what life is all about, folks. We fly so high, and we fade and die. Life is so short. It is just a vapor. Eternity is forever.

God's plan of salvation is very easy to understand:

- **Romans 3:23**
  For all have sinned and come short of the glory of God.

- **Romans 6:23**
  For the wages of sin is death; but the gift of God is eternal life through Jesus Christ our Lord.

- **John 1:12**
  But as many as receive him, to them gave he the power to become the sons of God, even to them that believe on his name.

- **Revelation 3:20**
  Behold I stand at the door and knock: If any man hear my voice, and open the door, I will come in to him, and will sup with him, and he with me.

God is good, and all He wants us to do is to admit that we are sinners and know that He is the only true and living God. Ask Him to forgive us of our sins, and let Him lead us through this life. After salvation, He wants us to make it public by baptism. Through His leadership, He will convict us when we do wrong, and then we must ask for His forgiveness and move on.

I am not saying that we must go overboard here and try to become holier than thou. Just follow God's simple plan to be a witness for Him, and live life to its fullest with a positive attitude. He has said that He would lead us through this life into that eternal home that He has prepared for us in heaven. This is between only us and God. No one else can do this for us. Jesus paid the price.

I have done this, and I hope and pray that you have, too. If so, I will see you in Heaven someday. Amen!

John Frye - 1963

Conclusion: The Next Book

I have certainly enjoyed writing this book. Now what is next? It looks like another book is coming, since I have already begun writing it.

Now that I have graduated from high school, let's make an assessment:

In 1963:

- John F. Kennedy was President of the U.S.
- Lyndon B. Johnson was Vice President.
- The Dow Jones was 767
- Unemployment was 5.5%
- A new house cost $19,300
- Gas was .30/gal.
- Eggs were .55/doz.
- Milk was .49/gal

Now I had a good education and still had my family, but there was still no money. I didn't have fifty cents to my name when I graduated in May 1963. I still had many **"Turns in Life"** coming in front of me. I did know that there was a God, but I didn't know much about how I was going to live yet.

I never had very much and seemed very satisfied at this point. I had a vision of a very simple life. I just wanted to be average. I wanted to grow up to be trustworthy, respected, and live a of life of integrity. Maybe someday I would have a loving family and a nice home in the city. I did not understand that I really had an opportunity to be whatever I wanted to be. Things were not clear. This may have been true because I had never had much of an opportunity to do anything in my life, except survive. Therefore, I didn't think I had the right to expect much more. It seemed like it wouldn't be fair for my family for me to expect more than they had in life.

Now, here I sit facing my computer, I just completed my first book. The date is August 18, 2013. It has taken me about a year to complete it. I wrote it in my spare time. I have not yet retired. I may do some more writing during my retirement years. Reliving the experiences has been a lot better than having to live through them the first time. I hope that this book remains in my family for many generations to come. And maybe, it will be enjoyed my many other readers also.

I have had the opportunity to work in the Multiwall Paper Bag Industry most of my life. It will be 50 years on May 18, 2014. I may write a special edition covering my bag plant experiences.

God has blessed me in so many ways. I am now 68 years old. I have a great family. Sue and I have been happily married for 46 years. I love her very much. She is my "Guardian Angel". God knew what I needed, and he sent her to me. I have a very nice home, a good church, and I am financially able to retire when I have a reason to. The **"Turns in Life"** have led me to this point.

The question is: Would I have changed anything? Probably not. Oh, if I had a nickel or two to put in that old pinball machine back at the corner store in Altheimer, that would have been great. God has blessed me in many ways, and he has led me through the **"Turns in Life"**. Thank you Lord!

What does this all mean? Success; Happiness; Security!

Matthew 16:26

For what is a man profited, if he shall gain the whole world, and lose his own soul?

I think we are all selfish by nature. We want everything for ourselves. We need to develop a desire to help others and to have a good testimony for God. We don't need to place too much confidence in people, for people will let you down. People can hurt you with words, they can physically hurt you, but no one can take away your salvation. That is between you and God and no one else.

We need to make sure we keep life in the right prospective. We need to live life to its fullest every day, pray to God for His forgiveness, and be ready to enter His kingdom in a flash.

Being the baby in the family has allowed me to out live all of my immediate family. Bill passed away very young. He was only 35 years old; Mother made it to 68; Louis, Buddy, and Louise all passed away in their 60s. Charles and Billy passed away early in life; they were both in their early fifties.

God has allowed me to live through a generation of great change. Travel is very convenient. We can go anywhere in the world in just a matter of hours. Communication has changed from the "party line" to the cell phone. Social Media has improved to the touch of a button. The Internet has given us more information than we could ever need.

In 2013:

- Barrack Obama – First minority President of the U.S.

- Joe Biden – Vice President

- Dow Jones – 15,000

- Unemployment rate – 7.4

- Gas - $3.35/gal.

- Eggs - $1.83/doz.

- Bread - $1.43/loaf

- Milk - $3.44/gal

I never could have imagined how much change could have taken place, just in my lifetime. Most of it has been in the last few years. Change is now on a rampage. In the early years, change took its time. Time sort of seemed to stand still for a while, but not any more.

In my next book, "**The Turns in Life**-After High School", I will review things such as:

- What about college?
- Family challenges.
- Work career.
- How religion finally gave me the boost that I needed.
- Marriage. (God did send me a guardian angel).
- A son
- Financial gain
- Grandkids
- Retirement

Made in the USA
Charleston, SC
10 February 2014